Psyche's Stories

Psyche's Stories

Modern Jungian Interpretations of Fairy Tales

EDITED BY MURRAY STEIN AND LIONEL CORBETT

Volume One

Chiron Publications
Asheville, North Carolina

2017 Paperback Edition, ISBN 978-1-63051-468-6

Grateful acknowledgment is made for permission to reprint "Male Naivete and the Loss of the Kingdom" (originally published in *Inroads*), © by Robert Bly.

Contents

Editors' Preface

This collection of essays presents a diversity of voices within a unified chorus. The unifying factor is analytical psychology, a network of theory and practical knowledge that has grown up around the thought and work of C. G. Jung. The diversity stems from each author's individual appropriation of that body of knowledge, but also from a particular set of personal life experiences and the freedom to write in a personally comfortable style.

Each essay interprets a fairy tale. Some of the tales are well known, others are not. The fairy tales have been selected by the authors to thematize and personify the play of universal intrapsychic and interpersonal dynamics and psychic contents. They are treated as dreams, not of individuals but of cultures, which arise from a timeless source of theme and image, the collective unconscious of humanity.

The sceptical reader may wonder whether the tales act merely as a sort of Rorschach stimulus for these authors, onto which they freely project their own fantasy images and thoughts, or whether the methods and theories of analytical psychology so prejudice the authors' thinking at the outset that the conclusions are foregone before any individual effort has been expended to trace meanings and significance. Both are possible pitfalls, which the authors have struggled to avoid. A common body of theory – analytical psychology – guards against the first menace, and the probing mind of each gifted author protects against the second. The authors presented here have done an admirable job in this regard.

The authors are all practicing psychotherapists and clinicians. Their concern for human beings and for the soul shines clearly through their written words. Each is seeking to discern, in a favorite fairy tale, something of the soul's essence for the practical purpose of enhancing life and illuminating the processes and struggles inherent in selfhood. The interpretations are as broad and deep, or as narrow and limited, as the authors' own experiences and understandings of the Self.

The tales themselves are inexhaustible and open to endless extensions of meaning and significance. Like the chromosomes in which our physiological blueprint is stored, fairy tales, in themselves, contain our psychological heritage. The archetypal contents and processes embedded in these tales have always been a part of the human psyche, and they continue to play an essential role in human development and wholeness. The meaning of any one such story is not fully expressible in language by any single author. The authors of these essays, aware of this limitation, would readily agree that much more could be said about each tale than they have conveyed here.

The editors wish to thank the authors for their enthusiastic labors in creating this volume of modern analytical interpretation. It has been a joy to receive these works and a wonder to behold their beauty and wealth of insights.

Murray Stein
Wilmette, Illinois

Lionel Corbett
Santa Fe, New Mexico

The Structural and Archetypal Analysis of Fairy Tales

Jole Cappiello McCurdy

INTRODUCTION

In "The Phenomenology of the Spirit in Fairy Tales" Jung writes that "the theory of the psychic structure was not derived from fairy tales and myths, but is grounded on empirical observations made in the field of medical-psychological research and was corroborated only secondarily through the study of comparative symbology, in spheres very far removed from ordinary medical practice" (1948, par. 432). Fairy tales are indeed so far removed that they almost immediately take us into another world, a fantastic, imaginary one, a world where everything is possible and unpredictable. Nonetheless, the two worlds – that of reality and that of fairy tales – apparently so different and so distant from one another, are as interconnected and complementary as the worlds of dreams and daylight. As products of the unconscious, dreams tell us what is in the background of our conscious lives; so fairy tales, as products of the creative fantasy, tell us about the various possible developments of our individual lives. Fairy tales stand to our historical and determined reality as a background of leitmotifs, as a world of possible happenings which may eventually characterize our lives. In fact, Jung saw fairy tales as containing the archetypal motifs – the basic patterns of development that unfold and actualize themselves through human consciousness. As Jung stressed, therefore, fairy tales can further illuminate and validate formulations derived from clinical observation.

The quote from Jung cited above emphasizes a method of analysis that, although essentially clinical in its premises, uses the products of the unconscious in order to amplify and deepen the understanding of the clinical material. Jung always stressed the fact that he was an empiricist and that he had come to the concept of the archetypes by observing and studying the human psyche in all its manifestations: normal, abnormal, creative; in symptoms, in dreams, and in insanity; and in comparative materials found in myths, fairy tales, art, and religion. Through clinical observation and the study of comparative material, Jung came to his concepts about the structure of the psyche and its basic patterns, the archetypes. He writes, "There *is* an *a priori* factor in all human activities, namely, the inborn, preconscious and unconscious individual structure of the psyche" (1954b, par. 151). And he continues, "Since everything psychic is preformed, this must also be true of the individual functions, especially those which derive directly from the unconscious predisposition. The most important of these is creative fantasy. In the products of fantasy the primordial images are made visible, and it is here that the concept of archetype finds its specific application" (ibid., par. 153).

Archetypes are patterns of behavior, modes of functioning of the human psyche similar to the instincts, that follow a distinct goal, the meaning of which becomes more and more clear as they unfold in their actual expressions or images. Their goal is to bring to consciousness, and therefore to transform, what was previously unconscious or preconscious. This process of development and transformation Jung called the individuation process.

Fairy tales, like fantastic productions, are closely related to the unconscious and its processes. In their typical structure, fairy tales picture the mode of functioning of the psyche and its goals. Analysis of the tale, from the Jungian point of view, leads to the isolation, identification, and study of archetypal patterns and to the process of individuation played out as a whole endowed with meaning. As the enactment of an intrapsychic process, portraying the encounter of the two realms, the conscious and the unconscious, the fairy tale, according to Jungian analysis, describes the process of individuation in its full complexity.

As first described classically by Jung, individuation is essentially a process of renewal and widening of the ego-consciousness.

It is in this classical sense that I refer to individuation here. As such, it presupposes an ego-consciousness already emerged from the unconscious background through a process of painful and progressive separation from the matrix, the collective unconscious, symbolized by the Mother. As a result of this separation, ego-consciousness gains a necessary distance from the unconscious, and thereby strengthens its boundaries. But, with increased distinctiveness and clarity, ego-consciousness progressively loses its contact with the unconscious matrix. There ensues a condition of imbalance between conscious and unconscious, a dissociation. Symptoms appear. Disconnected from its instinctual source, ego-consciousness is in danger of dying, of becoming rigid and sterile. Consequently, the ego must go back to the unconscious, to the collective matrix, in order to renew itself, to gain access to new archetypal energies and forms. The confrontation between the ego and the unconscious is, in essence, symbolized by the hero myths and tales, by the tales of death and rebirth. In its descent and journey, described by these myths, the ego encounters the various archetypes of the collective unconscious, and, as a result, ego-consciousness is renewed and progressively widened. Since, as von Franz states, every widening of consciousness has a healing effect, the previous condition of suffering and constriction is rectified (1970a, p. 10). Just so, the fairy tale, as we shall see, begins with a state of suffering and is resolved in the happy ending.

In her book, *The Interpretation of Fairy Tales* (1970b), von Franz points out that the different ways of looking at fairy tales may also be influenced by one of the four functions of consciousness. In particular, the thinking type will try to find in the tales some kind of structure or pattern underlying their diversity, tending then to formulate general rules or laws that govern these structures. The feeling type will be interested in developing value judgments about the tales. The sensation type will be most attached to a single image and will try to enrich and amplify the fairy tales' symbols. The intuitive will see the tale as a whole endowed with meaning, understanding it as a unique message (ibid., p. 11). Other factors besides typology can influence the way one sees a tale. Theoretical premises, personal experiences or projections, as well as motivations, are examples. One can see the tale as a reflection of a psychodynamic explanation or use the tale as a therapeutic tool. All these different approaches explain not only the variety and diversity of literature on fairy tales, but the limits of each as well.

But, for our purposes especially, the most important consideration is that fairy tales address a symbolic truth. Symbols do not exhaust themselves in one interpretation or in one meaning. Like crystals, symbols can be approached from many different angles and facets.

As a way of introducing single and detailed analyses of particular tales, I will consider a general pattern or structure of fairy tales themselves, a kind of ideal tale which can help us to identify an Ariadne thread in the complexity of all tales. Moveover, I am intent on seeing the fairy tale as symbolizing a univocal process, namely the individuation process as described by Jung. For these purposes, I will use Vladimir Propp's structural approach to fairy tales. As Jung did from a different point of view, this scholar saw fairy tales as a whole made up of different units strictly interrelated.

VLADIMIR PROPP AND THE STRUCTURAL ANALYSIS OF FAIRY TALES

Vladimir Propp, a Russian formalist writing in the 1920s, was reclaimed from near-obscurity by Claude Lévi-Strauss (Lévi-Strauss 1960), who further credited Propp's prophetic intuition as anticipating by a quarter-century Lévi-Strauss's own formulations on the structural analysis of myth (1955). Although in his work on the structure of fairy tales Propp's intention and goal were clearly very different from Jung's, we shall see, in examining Propp, that structural analysis of fairy tales both affirms and extends the Jungian analytic approach, thereby deepening our understanding of the psychic reality portrayed in the tale.

In his book, *Morphology of the Folk Tale*, Propp is concerned with the way in which the fairy tale is structured, with the interrelationships of the component parts, and with the relationship of the parts to the whole (1958, p. 1). Limiting his consideration to a particular group of fairy tales defined as tales of magic, in which a supernatural, extraordinary, miraculous, numinous element is always present, Propp abstracts various laws, concluding generally that, despite the variety of characters, of character traits, and of plot complexities, identical *functions* appear repeatedly in tale after tale. Functions for Propp are types of actions performed by the characters in the tale, meaningful and fateful actions, "defined from the point of view of [their] significance for the course of action of a tale as a whole" (ibid., p. 20). With the concept of function as basic, Propp formulates the following general principles of the structure of fairy tales:

1. Functions serve as stable, constant elements in folk tales, independent of who performs them, and how they are fulfilled by the *dramatis personae*. They constitute the components of a folk tale.
2. The number of functions known in the fairy tale is limited.
3. The sequence of functions is always identical.
4. All fairy tales, by their structure, belong to one and the same type. (ibid., pp. 20–21)

In the magical tale, the fairy tale of a numinous character (that which, in Jungian terms, derives from the archetypal level of the unconscious), Propp discerns consistent structures comprised of forms, or functions. These functions act as patterns of behavior, which follow a chronological succession and have meaning, or intentionality. That Propp's discoveries have important implications for the Jungian interpretation of fairy tales will become clearer as we proceed.

Propp first speaks of what he designates as the tale's "initial situation" (ibid., p. 24), which reveals the number and names of the personages and describes their characteristics and their roles. (Just as Jungians believe the dream's initial presentation is important, so also is the tale's initial situation.) Early in the tale, a state of lack or insufficiency, or, conversely, a state of abundance, exists. If there is abundance, there is also an atmosphere of tension which forebodes future misfortune; that misfortune in turn results in the condition of lack or deprivation. Propp describes actions leading to the misfortune which brings about the lack as the preparatory section of the tale.

The functions of this preparatory section are: (1) The absence, which describes the circumstances under which one of the cast of characters leaves home. Usually this character is the hero,* but others, such as the parents, may leave or die. Following the

*"Hero" is used here asexually, to connote male or female protagonist.

absence is (2) the interdiction. The hero receives an order or a simple request not to commit a certain action. In response there is (3) the violation of the interdiction. As a consequence of this violation (4) the villain or antagonist appears in the tale. Often the villain (5) turns up first in disguised form, for example, as the thief who pretends to be a beggar. The villain then (6) tries to entice or lure the hero into revealing information that the villain needs. The victim (hero) next (7) "submits to deception and thereby unwittingly helps his enemy" (ibid., p. 28). Propp calls this last function "complicity" (ibid.). The complicity can be accomplished by explicit consent or simply by falling asleep at the most dangerous moment. Although passive, falling asleep nevertheless "facilitates the villain's dirty work." In any case, the breaking of the interdiction leads to (8) the condition of misfortune, damage, or lack mentioned above, which in turn calls for (9) the intervention of the hero.

As we have pointed out, the condition of lack may already exist when the tale opens. It may manifest simply as a desire for something missing, such as the childless royal couple wanting an heir. In those tales where villainy creates the misfortune, the villainy itself can take diverse forms—abduction, murder, stealing, bewitching, etc. (The beginning may be insidious or acute, as so commonly happens in the human situation.) Regardless, the effect is always the same: the resulting deprivation or damage requires a quest by the hero.

At this point, we encounter the ninth function—heroic intervention: "misfortune or shortage is made known: the hero is either approached with a request and responds to it of his own accord, or is commanded and dispatched" (ibid., p. 33). There are two types of heroes in fairy tales: the active, or seeker, hero and the victim hero. For example, if the princess is kidnapped and Ivan goes in search of her, Ivan is a seeker hero. But if the princess is kidnapped, and the tale then follows her in all her misadventures and trials, then the princess is a victim hero. If the hero is a seeker, a tenth function follows: "The seeker agrees to or decides upon counteraction." The decision to respond to the call implies a volitional act, and it is only characteristic of seeker heroes. The victim hero is another story, and I find fascinating and extremely important what Propp writes about the victim heroes: "banished, vanquished, bewitched and substituted heroes demonstrate no volitional aspiration toward freedom" (ibid., p.

35). In psychological terms, in the victim hero we have a description of total possession or regression.

Whether victim or seeker, the hero leaves home (11). For the seeker hero this departure means the beginning of a search; for the victim hero, the beginning of a series of sufferings. At this point a new character enters the tale: the donor or, more precisely, the provider. Usually the provider is encountered accidentally, on the road or in the wood, for example. But, before providing help, the donor tests the hero (12) in various ways. She or he may demand of the hero a long period of sacrifice or that seemingly impossible tasks be performed. The donor may appear as a prisoner and require that the hero free him or her. (This particular example will be of special interest later when we discuss the archetypal interpretation of the figure of the donor.) In other instances, the donor asks simply to be recognized as such and given credit for his or her importance, even if she or he appears in ridiculous, powerless, inferior, or animal form. Whatever the specifics, the hero must recognize the importance of the donor, react to the request (13), and accomplish the tasks the donor demands. Only after having given clear evidence of the worth of his or her own qualities and abilities will the hero receive from the donor the magical means (14) that will help to counter the original villainy. Although the characteristics, nature, and mode of transmission of the magical means can differ markedly from one tale to another, the function of the magical means remains the same: to provide the unexpected and extraordinary help the hero needs to accomplish the difficult quest.

Next, the hero reaches the place where the main deeds will take place (15), coming upon the castle where the princess is imprisoned, for example, or where the sinister antagonist reigns. There the hero will come into direct combat with the enemy (16) and, during the confrontation, will incur a wound (17), a mark signifying the act of courage. Marked by a symbol of this heroic gesture, the hero will be somewhat changed. (This function, stressing that the hero is transformed in the confrontation with the antagonist, is also very meaningful psychologically, as we will see.)

As a result of the direct combat, "the villain is defeated (18), and the initial misfortune or lack is liquidated (19)" (ibid., p. 48). An enchantment is broken, poverty is ended, a slain person is revived with the water of life. However, despite the hero's victory and the correction of the initial damaged or insufficient state, the tale does not necessarily end. Often, the hero's quest is not yet finished.

Carrying the mark of distinction acquired in combat, the hero returns home (20), but there is pursued or is not recognized or is banished by a false hero (21). Here the theme of sibling or rival jealousy seems to be dominant. Now, again, the hero must perform other impossible tasks or in some way prove his or her value or identity (25). Once again the task is accomplished, and the villain – now in the character of false hero or family member – is punished and definitively eliminated. Only at this point in the tale does the hero receive full recognition and a new rank. Propp gives this function (29) the name of "transfiguration" (ibid., p. 56). The last functions of the fairy tale are the marriage and the ascension to the throne which sanctions the process of transformation of the hero. With that, the tale ends.

Propp identified a total of thirty-one functions in the fairy tale. Naturally, not all the functions are present in every tale. Some isolated functions may be missing, for example, the preparatory section may not appear, or the tale may end when the initial villainy is countermanded. The important fact is that the relationship between functions is always the same; that is, the basic structure is always present. This structure gives a characteristic unity to the tales, a whole in which the intrinsic dynamic process is inherent as well as predictable. The structure unfolds in a stepwise manner, as a goal-directed process, as a pattern endowed with meaning. Furthermore, this network of functions is constant whether or not the tale's cast includes all of the seven different kinds of typical characters which Propp names. These seven – the villain, the donor, the helper, the sought-for person, the dispatcher, the hero, and the false hero – are identified according to their *functions*, not according to their attributes, motivations, or feelings. As Bruno Bettelheim expresses it, "All characters are typical rather than unique" (1977, p. 8). If, for example, the helper or donor is missing, his function may be transferred to the hero, who then assumes prophetic qualities. What is important is the *meaning* of the character's deed, not his identity (Propp 1958, pp. 79–82).

The above constitutes a brief summary of Propp's work and ideas, simplifying considerably their complexity and omitting many aspects which would be irrelevant for this discussion. Briefly recapitulating those aspects which are relevant, we want to remember that the tale of magic begins with a condition of lack and ends with restitution, liberation, marriage, or transformation. Between the beginning and the end, we find a series of events that are interconnected and constitute a stepwise process or movement. This is the common, basic structure, or morphology, of the fairy tale as Propp describes it.

Writers following Propp drew upon and expanded his ideas. Lévi-Strauss exceeded Propp in stressing that the content of the myth or tale is just as important as its structure because the content can itself reveal structure. The fact, for example, that a bird in a tale is an eagle, rather than an owl, is very significant: eagle and owl can represent an opposition, as in day and night. Even the tale's language, which Lévi-Strauss termed "metalanguage" and Jungians term "symbolic language," is critical, with every image standing for something else or something more. We are indebted to Lévi-Strauss, too, for the notion that myths can be read as musical compositions, with both horizontal and vertical sense, revealing identical themes repeated again and again in variation. Von Franz refers to something similar when she writes,

> In the unconscious all the archetypes are contaminated with one another. It is as if several photographs were printed one over the other; they cannot be disentangled. This has probably to do with the relative timelessness and spacelessness of the unconscious. It is as a package of representations which are simultaneously present. (1970b, p. 10)

This is the diachronic dimension of myth and fairy tales, the dimension that is out of time and space, the "once upon a time" dimension.

Lévi-Strauss further departed from Propp in that he was concerned principally with myth, as opposed to fairy tales. Myth, Lévi-Strauss believed, was more fitted for structural analysis than were tales because myths are organized according to a more rigorous internal logic, religious orthodoxy, and collective expectation. Fairy tales, he contended, contained greater freedom of expression and artistic creation. For precisely those reasons, von Franz believes that the tale is more appropriate than myth for the study of archetypal themes: being less formally structured, fairy tales are closer to the collective unconscious.

STRUCTURAL AND ARCHETYPAL ANALYSIS OF THE FAIRY TALE

At the time when Jung was formulating the concept of the archetype from his studies of the processes which govern the nature and structure of the psyche, Propp synchronistically was seeking to abstract general structural laws governing the morphology of the fairy tale. What Propp saw in an externalized, projected form, Jung recognized as an introjected and intrapsychic process. We will now see how comparable are these different ways of approaching the same material, and how much a structural analysis can add to our psychological understanding of fairy tales.

To begin with, we can consider the fact that Propp chose for his structural analysis a particular kind of tale – tales of magic. It is in these tales that he found a common basic structure. From a Jungian psychological point of view this is not surprising. Tales of magic all contain a supernatural element. They are most like myths in that they deal with the divine, the semidivine, the numinous element – that is, the unconscious. It is to the unconscious as matrix, as preexistent, timeless, and indefinite, unknown and never completely knowable, that the attributes of the divine and numinous belong. There belong the spirits, the gods, the witches, the magical power. And it is in the unconscious as matrix and precondition that the basic structure lies.

Tales of magic, therefore, speak to us about the unconscious, about this unknown other, the source of our major fears and major hopes. Fairy tales describe the steps of this encounter between known and unknown and indicate, by means of what Propp calls functions and what Jung calls archetypes, a way to confront, withstand, and win the power of the unconscious. The tale prepares us by anticipating our fears and desires and our responses to them. The tale is a projection into the future, a plan, something new to attain, entailing all the trepidation associated with acquiring something precious, the treasure which previously belonged to the unconscious. When we look at how this plan unfolds in light of both Propp's and Jung's theories, we see that the fairy tale is a symbolic expression of the personal quest, a quest that has as its goal the achievement of a higher personality and the development of a wider consciousness.

Propp states that the fairy tale begins with an initial situation which often describes a condition of imbalance: in a story about a father and three sons, the feminine element is lacking;

where there is a father and three daughters, the mother is missing; the sick or dying king lacks the water of life; and so on. If the lack is not immediately apparent, we will remember that the preparatory section of the tale leads to the insufficiency through the absence, the interdiction, and the violation of the interdiction which is followed by the villainy. From a psychological point of view, the condition of insufficiency, lack, or villainy describes the beginning of a neurotic symptomatology which comes about after a perturbation of the psychic equilibrium. The conditions existing at the beginning of the tale are equivalent to that individual state where a unilaterality of consciousness prevails: for example, the one-sided masculinity represented by the father and three sons mentioned above. Jung says that when this unilaterality exists – when the conscious and unconscious are no longer in dialectical opposition – it is then that symptoms appear.

With the appearance of symptoms, the unconscious begins its disturbing influence; at the same time, consciousness becomes more rigid in order to defend itself. On one side, we have in the tale, following Propp, the interdiction – representing the attempt at conscious defense – and, on the other side, we have the actions of the villain, representing the unconscious now perceived as an enemy. The hero – the ego – finds itself assaulted from two sides: from one side by the moral and rigid interdictions that constitute the persona and, from the other, by the pressure of the unconscious. The hero tries to defend himself or herself, but the villain tests and lures, undermining the defenses. Finally, the hero, explicitly or implicitly, will assent to the villain, giving in to the temptations that come from the unknown other.

It is interesting that Propp calls this function "complicity." We recall the story of the Fall, of Eve's and Adam's willingness to eat the forbidden fruit. The violation of the interdiction in fact represents the first actively heroic gesture of the hero. With the violation, contact with the unknown other, with the unconscious, is established and the process of development can now begin.

The complicity of the hero results in the temporary victory of the unconscious, and its negative influence becomes visible. Clinically, this stage is expressed in the full manifestation of the neurotic condition with its symptoms, its depression and anxiety. Through suffering, the hero, or ego, now becomes fully aware of the dangers of the unconscious; but it is only because of the pain and depression that the hero will resolve to begin the quest. One needs to touch the bottom before beginning the fight and the ascent. Propp in his analysis of fairy tales expresses this truth by pointing out that it is the lack which elicits the actions of the hero.

The quest, or journey, has as its goal the restitution of the villainy and victory over the unconscious. We should recall here that Propp distinguishes between two types of heroes, the seeker and the victim. His differentiating between these two heroic attitudes has great clinical validity. In working with analysands, one often encounters those who don't have any aspiration for freedom. Passive and hopeless, they seem to be possessed wholly by their unconscious complexes. In these cases, the analyst is forced to work against a total lack of reaction. What makes these victims heroes is their persistence, their enduring the suffering and pain inflicted by the unconscious. They don't give up. They are like reeds bent by all the winds, but never broken. Their particular quest lies in the strength of their natures, rather than in their actions.

The quest having been undertaken, the hero then meets the donor. We recall that it is the donor who will give the hero the magical means to overcome the enemy. The donor figure may be an animal, or a meaningless or funny being, or a scary, unpredictable, strange, and tricky being. Jung states that in the personal quest, in the individuation process, the ego first encounters its own shadow. Although it sums up all those qualities considered inferior and undeveloped by the collective consciousness, the shadow, which is either repressed, suppressed, denied, or undeveloped, is that aspect of the personality closest to the unconscious. That the donor can be understood as the shadow is corroborated by the fact that in many fairy tales the donor has something in common with the hero.

Or, we may see in the donor the archetypal trickster, which is also a shadow figure. Half human and half animal, half god, grotesque, funny, or terrifying, but still extremely clever, the trickster functions as a mediator between the unconscious and the conscious. Lévi-Strauss writes, "Thus the mediating function of the trickster explains that since its position is halfway between two polar terms, he must retain something of that duality, namely an ambiguous and equivocal character" (1955, p. 102). What is being described is the mercurial function. The shadow and the trickster know the unconscious; they know its dangers and powers. Therefore, being able to deal with the shadow or trickster means being able to see the paradoxical nature of the unconscious, its creative as well as its destructive nature. Only by dealing with Propp's donor will the hero be able to gain the magical means, that is, only by dealing with the shadow will the ego be able to appropriate some of the power of the unconscious. By analyzing the shadow, we are able to free some of the psychic energy imprisoned in it, energy which can then be used for our conscious realization. It is especially interesting that some of the donors in fairy tales are prisoners whom the hero must free.

After meeting, the donor first tests the hero. Having already encountered the unconscious as villain, the hero now is aware of the dangers of the unconscious and, this time, is ready to give the unconscious full recognition. The hero therefore bends before the supreme authority of the unconscious, and thus gains its favor: the magical means. Having obtained the magical means, the hero enters into direct combat with the villain, thereby repairing the initial villainy. Psychologically, this means that the ego, after its confrontation with the shadow, is able to face and overcome the dominance of the unconscious. Clinically, this step leads to the disappearance of symptoms and the establishment of a new equilibrium between conscious and unconscious.

The fairy tale, and the analysis, could end here, for the task has been accomplished, and the damage has been repaired. The encounter with the shadow, with all that was repressed and suppressed, has resulted in the disappearance of symptoms. In some fairy tales, once the villainy has been repaired, the hero, for example, returns home, meets a princess, and marries her. Jung states, "to the degree to which the shadow is recognized and integrated, the problem of the anima, i.e., of relationship, is constellated" (1954a, par. 485). The encounter with the anima/animus represents a further stage in the individuation process. Now the individual, no longer gripped by symptoms or depression, nor oppressed by guilt or the shadow, begins to feel again, to become animated, to look around. Something inside becomes alive and active. This spark is the soul, the anima/animus archetype, which seeks connection, relationship. It seeks the opposite, both in intrapsychic and in interpersonal relationships, with which it longs to unite. This step in the individuation process is also the most complicated one, because the imperative of relating to the opposite simultaneously vies with the intense desire for union. For these reasons, the pain, suffering, and debilitating quest for the other are so often portrayed in the tales.

Taking into account the entire range of functions identified by Propp, we see that some fairy tales can express the individuation process in its full complexity. You will recall that during the combat with the villain the hero often receives a mark. She or he is now different: the confrontation with the unconscious has been a deep and profound experience. The hero has come to know that the task was not only to bring to light what had been repressed; in the unconscious the hero has experienced endless and magic possibilities, things that consciousness never knew before. Similarly, for many analysands the quest cannot stop at the time when the symptoms disappear, or when the personal unconscious has been analyzed. Not everything in dreams can be analyzed reductively. We learn that our fantasies and dreams go far beyond our personal lives. And so the quest continues, this time taking on a more collective dimension.

The hero, after returning home, is not recognized. She or he meets the figure of the false hero, encounters the resistance of family and courtiers. Symbolically, these events point to the resistance the hero finds in the collectivity, to the hostilities one encounters when one wants to be different from the masses. To undergo a process of individuation means to be individual, to experience and live individually what is unconsciously collective, not to accommodate one's individuality to the collective. Therefore, the returning hero often is not recognized; often the hero will be persecuted if she or he refuses to conform to collective standards. Additional tasks are required. Meaningfully, this time the enemy may be hiding behind someone very familiar – a brother, a sister, a member of the court. Like the earlier villain, these enemies also belong to the unconscious, because everything representing mass attributes bear the same qualities of unconsciousness.

Eventually, the hero's individual value is recognized by the bestowal of a new rank, followed by the hero's transfiguration, and, finally, a marriage. These are accompanied by the final defeat of the villain. The recognition and transfiguration express the fact that the hero, through the individual task, has affected the collective consciousness: his or her message has finally gotten through, and the collective consciousness has appropriated for itself something divine and supernatural. In fact, in the individuation process, the ego, by confronting and coming to terms with both the collective unconscious and the collective conscious, acquires a new position, one which does not belong to either, but is part of both realms. The new rank, the new connotation the hero/ego acquires is that of the Self, the new ruler. As von Franz writes: "Only with the attainment of the Self are the shadow and the anima really won, because only then does the situation become stabilized" (1970b, p. 17). The perfect harmony that ensues between conscious and unconscious is symbolized by the marriage, that is, the *coniunctio.*

Thus the fairy tale, in the full expression of all its functions as described by Propp and as analyzed from a Jungian point of view, is the expression of a process of evolution, of change, of improvement and enrichment of the initial situation. By analogy, the process of individuation, which begins in a condition of suffering and neurotic decompensation, leads not only to restitution, but to progressive enlargement of the personality. For these reasons, Jung saw symptoms and neurosis as potentially positive conditions, since it is through them that the whole individuation process begins. From a mood, a depression, a painful state, the quest begins, and, once begun, it is directed not only backward to the repressed shadow, but also forward, bringing to light unknown and not yet experienced potentialities hiding in the unconscious. That is the fairy tale's happy ending.

REFERENCES

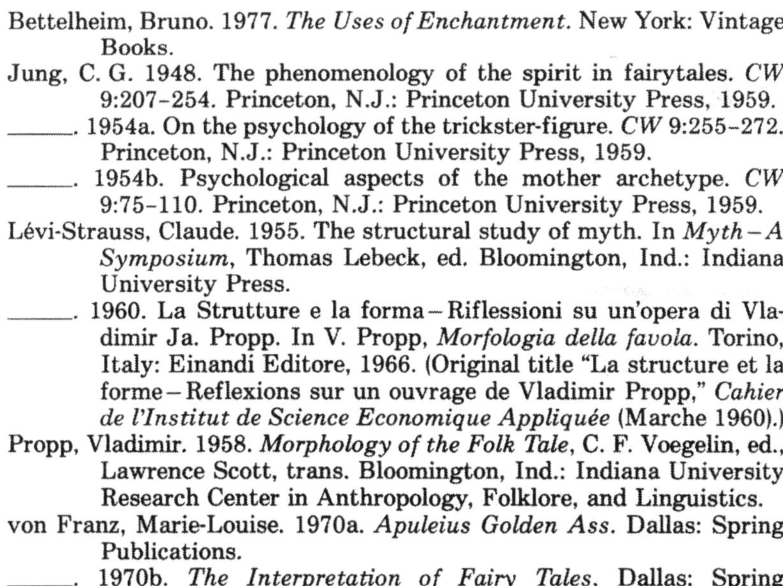

Bettelheim, Bruno. 1977. *The Uses of Enchantment.* New York: Vintage Books.

Jung, C. G. 1948. The phenomenology of the spirit in fairytales. *CW* 9:207–254. Princeton, N.J.: Princeton University Press, 1959.

______. 1954a. On the psychology of the trickster-figure. *CW* 9:255–272. Princeton, N.J.: Princeton University Press, 1959.

______. 1954b. Psychological aspects of the mother archetype. *CW* 9:75–110. Princeton, N.J.: Princeton University Press, 1959.

Lévi-Strauss, Claude. 1955. The structural study of myth. In *Myth – A Symposium*, Thomas Lebeck, ed. Bloomington, Ind.: Indiana University Press.

______. 1960. La Strutture e la forma – Riflessioni su un'opera di Vladimir Ja. Propp. In V. Propp, *Morfologia della favola.* Torino, Italy: Einandi Editore, 1966. (Original title "La structure et la forme – Reflexions sur un ouvrage de Vladimir Propp," *Cahier de l'Institut de Science Economique Appliquée* (Marche 1960).)

Propp, Vladimir. 1958. *Morphology of the Folk Tale*, C. F. Voegelin, ed., Lawrence Scott, trans. Bloomington, Ind.: Indiana University Research Center in Anthropology, Folklore, and Linguistics.

von Franz, Marie-Louise. 1970a. *Apuleius Golden Ass.* Dallas: Spring Publications.

______. 1970b. *The Interpretation of Fairy Tales.* Dallas: Spring Publications.

"Allerleirauh" (All-Kinds-of-Fur) A Tale of Father Dominance, Psychological Incest, and Female Emergence

Julia Jewett

Familial incest, whether overt or covert (that is, actual physical violation or intrusive innuendo), is a common fact of many life histories brought for therapeutic hearing. Always distressing, disturbing, these transgressions of the ancient taboo range from the "kiss Daddy goodnight" variety to brutal and sadistic encounters. Each instance is unique, yet there are similarities among individuals in the way psyche structures itself around the event, so that souls who have experienced incest recognize one another's resultant patterning. No matter what the gender or generational pairing, there are, seemingly, similar results in the patterning of personality. These patterns are equally (although sometimes more obscurely) evident in instances of what I call "psychological incest." Psychological incest is the deviation from ascribed and boundaried family positions in order to join another *inappropriately* to one's enterprise. In the tale we are about to consider, the powerful father (king) seeks to wed his daughter in order to provide a queen for the realm and thereby, presumably, restore order. However, incest of whatever stripe begets only *dis*order. Psychological incest, colloquially put, would say: "You and me, kid, we'll take care of this together." What results is the subversion of the daughter's developing true self. As with other forms of incest, there results a very strong bonding between victim and other, a deep sense of mistrust of others, and a lack of developed self as though time had stopped at the moment of bonding, sending the true self into hiding, allowing only an adaptive persona to continue interacting with the world. The true self may have any number of characteristics depending on the individual, but it will *at least* be typified by concealment, camouflage, and a somewhat flighty coming and going in its evidence both to others and to its own ego-self. With these initial comments in mind, hear a recapitulation of the tale.

Allerleirauh (All-Kinds-of-Fur)

There once was a king whose beautiful, golden-haired wife became ill unto death. But before she died, she made the king promise that if he should wish to marry again, he must have only a bride as beautiful and golden-haired as she. For a time the king grieved and did not think to remarry, but soon his councilors convinced him that a queen was needed for the realm.

The king beheld his grown daughter, now the image of her mother. Falling violently in love, he vowed to wed her. The councilors, aghast, exclaimed that the kingdom would be brought down in the face of such sin. The daughter, even more dismayed, concocted a plan that she thought impossible for him to fulfill. She asked for three dresses, one as golden as the sun, one as silvery as the moon, and one as glittering as the stars. Further, she demanded a cloak made of a thousand kinds of fur, a pelt from every animal in the realm. But the dresses were skillfully woven and the cape was created; then the king announced the forthcoming wedding.

Now there was nothing left but for the young princess to run away. From among her treasures she took three things: a gold ring, a tiny gold spinning wheel, and a tiny gold reel. She placed the three dresses of the sun, moon, and stars into a nutshell, blackened her hands and face with soot, put on the fur cape, and departed. Commending herself to God, she walked the whole night into a forest and fell asleep in the hollow of a tree. There she was sniffed out by the hunting dogs of the king of that forest and seized. She protested, "I'm a poor child, forsaken by father and mother. Have pity on me and take me with you," and she was carried off to the royal palace. She was given a cubbyhole under the stairs where no light of day penetrated and set to the multiple tasks of the scullery. There she lived wretchedly for a long time.

In time, a ball was given at the palace, and Allerleirauh was allowed to go upstairs for a short time. Removing her fur pelts and washing so that her full beauty shone forth, she put on the golden dress, entered the dance like the king's daughter that she was, entranced the king of this palace, and then disappeared. Returning to her cubby hole, she hid her fine dress, blackened her hands and face, donned her cloak of a thousand furs, and then was instructed by the cook to make the king's bread pudding so that the cook, too, could ascend to enjoy the party. The cook cautioned her not to let a single hair fall in the pudding, and she did not, but instead placed her gold ring in the bottom of the bowl. When the king discovered this token, he was dumbfounded. He called the cook and demanded to know who had prepared the pudding. When the cook claimed to have done it, the king denounced him, "for it was a different kind and much better cooked than usual." At this, the cook confessed that Allerleirauh had made it, and she was sent for. When the king inquired, "Who are you?" and "Why are you in my palace?" she repeated "I'm a poor child who no longer has either a father or a mother" and added, "I'm good for nothing but to have boots thrown at my head." She declined any knowledge of the ring, and so the king let her go.

Twice more a ball was held and each time Allerleirauh appeared briefly and then retreated to the scullery to make a remarkable bread pudding. The second time she wore the moon-silver dress and dropped the gold spinning wheel in the bowl. The third time she wore her starry-blue dress and put the golden reel in the pudding. However, on the occasion of the third dance, the king slipped a gold ring on her finger, and when she returned to her cubby hole, she carelessly left one finger white and unsooted. When, as usual, she was called before the king to account for the delicious food, her white finger and the king's gold ring marked her. As she tried to run away, a glimpse of her starry dress showed through an opening in the cloak, and she could no longer conceal herself. The king flung the cloak away, her golden hair appeared, she wiped the ashes from her face and appeared in her full beauty. The king claimed her for his bride, the wedding was celebrated, and they lived happily forever.

In briefly analyzing this tale, we have to say at the outset that the first king is stuck in one narrow ego perception. He cannot imagine any woman other than an exact replacement of his dead queen. The phrase (in reference to his daughter) "In every respect she was like his dead wife" suggests to me the projection of an anima ideal, leaving her no room for differentiation, personal uniqueness, for self. In the outer situation of the king, his capitulation to his dying wife's demands and his subsequent clinging to that agreement cause him to appear henpecked, unimaginative, dependent. In an interior view, we see the soul's lifelessness that is the hallmark of an anima problem. We see, in fact, that he was so unattuned to life that his councilors (presumably an internal advisory council in his psyche) had to be the ones to initiate action.

But the girl is our chief concern, and it is when her father chooses her for his queen that her true self becomes frozen in time; the circumstances make no room for *her* choice, wishes, uniqueness, and so forth. That is the horror of incest: like rape, it treats the female as an object and can turn her psychology toward a victim position. At this point, Allerleirauh takes her fate upon herself with two moves. First she tries to divert her father by asking for what looks like the impossible. Interestingly, these objects, the three dresses and the cloak of a thousand furs which seemed impossible, later become the means of possibility for her *with a different king*. Her second move is to leave, and this is no mean feat. In actuality, whether incest has taken place or strong psychological bonding exists, it is hard for the daughter to leave. Once the king's eye has fallen upon her, it is as though a marriage has already taken place. But this young woman is able to leave, and she takes with her what is small enough to carry and seemingly essential to her.

Her disguise is the key to understanding this story, and it is here that I want to introduce the element of initiation. In ritual initiation, it is the custom for the initiate to be forced from home under frightening circumstances, to disguise themselves, hiding their former identity, to enter a hidden space, to endure trials, and finally to emerge with a new identity, never to return to the former way. Allerleirauh's disguise is her cape of furs; her hidden space is first the tree hollow, then the scullery where she endures lightless living space and menial tasks under a harsh master (the cook) before emerging as a newly evolved self.

One of the first parts of this initiation is the denial of family: "I am a poor girl who no longer has any father or mother." This renunciation of former identifying ties has a scriptural parallel in Jesus' repudiation of family: "My mother and brothers are those who hear the word of God and do it" (Luke 8:21). We can see this young woman as involved in a process of self-initiation – so common today in the absence of culturally affirmed ritual process – as she instinctively follows the Self's urgings in an individuation process. Here the psychological instinct toward individuation is complicated by the father's wish to pervert physical instinctuality. Yet as we shall see, the adage "in the symptom lies the seed of cure of the neurosis" prevails. For Allerleirauh's disguise is the very emblem of instinctuality. She is cloaked specifically in *animal pelts* which would suggest that she is not only carrying the instinctual life with her, she is in fact enveloped by it. How like a complex! We must also notice that the room she inhabits is in the basement of the castle (or as we might say, in the unconscious). It is described as "a closet under the stairs where no daylight entered." This is an apt description of depression, and it seems so often that the discomfort of this dark mode of soul is what impels a person toward consciousness.

Now comes the series of comings and goings, of partial disclosings, of her tokens in the bowl as obscure intimations that something is afoot that is other than what it seems. I have wondered about the role of the cook. It seems that, psychologically, in the situation of a hidden true self, there is another factor in psyche who I call "the one who sniffs the air and tells if it's safe here." This is an enabling figure, one who harbors the true self and facilitates its slow emergence. In this story, the cook helps Allerleirauh's true worth to be seen by the new king; he has her cook the pudding and then has to admit that it was she who made it so well.

Another notable feature of the tale is that each time the king asks her about the object found in the bottom of the bowl, Allerleirauh claims to know nothing. Pondering this, I think we can take that as the truth. When the true self is still in hiding in the unconscious, it is as unavailable to the individual's ego consciousness as it is to everyone else. In fact, evidence of it – little glimpses like these tokens in the bowl – often are more visible to others than to the one who is in the process of transformation. When this elusive coming and going of the true self is in phase, it really does look like a furtive animal now showing itself to sniff the air, then diving back underground again. The king's rapid gesture of putting a gold ring on her finger fits the motif perfectly, for he "tagged" her in just the way that is done with wild animals who are to be tracked. Perhaps he did care enough to track her patterns, and she trusted enough – or the watchguard in her psyche did – to think this might be safe space. Maybe, finally, someone really does care about her.

The three objects she took with her when she first departed her father's household – the ring, the spindle and the reel – are major factors in her eventual emergence and are symbolic. As such, they are intriguing and suggestive – truly, as Jung would have it, the best possible statement – but elusive of any definitive interpretation. One idea that has been put forward is that the three objects taken together form a trinary image of transformation using the stages in the weaving process (Lee Roloff, in conversation). From undifferentiated wholeness (ring), the yarn gathers around the spindle (formation of complex), and finally is transferred to the reel where it is held in an organized fashion, ready to create material. In this image, the process of individuation is outlined simply: the thread originates in the Self, forms a complex over time, and eventually becomes conscious, enlarging the personality as it is integrated. As with any weaving project, it is necessary to keep a sensitive tension so that the outcome is smooth without loopy or loose stitches nor breaking with tautness. This is the genius of the psyche in the process of transformation. Given optimum circumstances, the psyche is self-regulating, giving us what we need when we need it. The emergence of Allerleirauh as a feminine self seems to be a product of natural tension just as the formation of fabric comes from the loom in regulated stages.

Another take on the imagery of ring, spindle, and reel is tied to the central issue of incest. In the image of incest, it is the feminine self that is violated specifically by way of sexual threat. It is exactly her essential sexual self that Allerleirauh is trying to protect by leaving her father. Ring, spindle, and reel are each in their essential movement circular, suggesting generally female roundedness but specifically the rotating or gyrating movement of the female in sexual intercourse. Perhaps her act of putting these out for the king, one by one, is a test whether in this instance she can be valued rather than subsumed in her essential femaleness. This bodily sexual aspect of her feminine self is what was previously at risk with her father and therefore is the tender place where healing must occur.

A composite picture of such a woman begins with the reality of the father complex which is enormously ambivalent. On the positive side, she has been "daddy's best girl," admired and made special; negatively, she has been so bonded to his image of her that her natural self has gone into hiding. There may be a well-developed persona and substantial success in the world of work but there is a gap like a Saturn ring between the outer persona adaptation and the hidden inner self. The therapeutic task is to reweave the fabric of the personality where this emptiness developed. Clearly the relationship with the personal mother is very damaged or nonexistent, since if the mother was "dead" to the king, she was equally dead to her daughter. As in any form of incest, the mother did not protect the daughter, so she has nothing of substance from the personal mother, relating to the world of the feminine. This is reflected in the tale by the fact that there are no other female figures in the tale except for Mother Nature which is protection at the archetypal level. It is commonly true that when there is inadequate input at the personal level, a woman's only recourse is to go to the archetypal level. In the initial stages of analysis these women's dreams are full of archetypal imagery, very helpful and supportive. However, the presence of the archetypal can be a problem, creating the potential for grandiosity and idealization. The three ball dresses may represent this tendency, linked as they are to the sun, moon and stars. If the father is made godlike, the child will likely carry an unconscious inflation by her proximity to the "great one."

Much of the weaving that has to be done centers on the area of the underdeveloped feminine, and that includes – finally – the development of a distinct personal style. This is reflected in the tale by the pudding that she makes which is not only perceived as good but recognized immediately as different from the one that the usual cook makes. What she makes has its own distinct flavor.

In her relationships with men, this woman duplicates exactly the tale's motif of "coming and going." There is a deep ambivalence about what is male because she has experienced her very selfhood threatened by its blindness toward her individuality and its entrenchment in its own need and narrow vision. At the same time, it is that force, that father force, that adored her single-mindedly and would give her anything her imagination could dream up. This is the terrible concrete glue of the father bonding in psychological incest. His godlike capacity to surround her, to clothe her in archetypally endowed raiment lends to the personal father the qualities of a god. What this does in psyche is to set up an amalgamation of personal and archetypal that is rock solid.

Until this father bond is broken (and it is usually so solid as to remain unconscious for a long time), she cannot truly be united with the masculine in a balanced way, inner *or* outer. This woman will likely say of her personal father, "Oh yes, well, he was all I had . . . he was the one who was there for me . . . he encouraged me, yes, yet there was also always the feeling that I should be like my mother." Very confusing.

In her relationship with a man she will not be quite all there. Her body will, by instinct, respond to sexual union, but it will not be true union because her soul is locked up. A verse from an old popular song says it nicely: "While tearing off a game of golf, I may make a play for the caddy. But when I do, I don't follow through because my heart belongs to Daddy" (Cole Porter, 1973). She attends to her daily life, but if he whistles, she comes running. Or, she may spend a lot of time denying his importance. At least the persona does. Underneath the outer facade or protests of devotion lies a deep rage that likely will not come out initially toward the personal father. Rather, her target will be cultural representations of the patriarch, usually institutions first. The church is in for it, as is any *perceived* collective stronghold of power. She will pick up a power complex in a man across a crowded room and she will both loathe and feel lured toward him. If she can, she will avoid him because she feels her own natural strength threatened by him. In fact, for quite a while she will tell you that she has no power and no power needs. She will dismiss the notion of women having any phallic power because the phallic reality has been so hurtful to her. And because this psychological condition is so prevalent in the culture, she may stay unnecessarily stuck because she gets a great deal of support for her position from women friends who have been similarly hurt. But eventually the rage will come out, and it has its place in cleansing the wound. But it does not depotentiate the complex. I know of no more powerful rage statement than Sylvia Plath's poem, "Daddy." This violent attempt to free herself failed; within six months of its writing she was dead, a suicide.

The tale gives the way out of the complex's grip in the image of sacrifice. Allerleirauh sacrifices the so-called protection of the father bond and enters the world of wandering, of journey, of strange places and questionable welcome. She sacrifices her status as a princess and potential queen for the condition of servitude. Chiefly, she enters the place of aloneness. In this space a woman must reckon with her own soul, doing only what she must to subsist, spending most of her energy in *being* rather than *doing*, in solitude, in reflection. Traditionally, women have gone from their father's protection to that of a husband without the initiatory step of aloneness in between. Still, psyche will find a way to confront us with the need for evolution. As Jung says, "The natural course of life demands that the young person should sacrifice his childhood and his childish dependence on the personal parents, lest he remain caught body and soul in the bonds of *unconscious incest*" (Jung 1952, par. 553. Italics mine). A key notion in this phrase is the sacrifice of childhood. The victim of incest, whether physical or psychological, has experienced arrested development at whatever age this violence began. Jung has also stated, "unconscious self-sacrifice is merely an accident, not a moral act" (Jung 1954, par. 400). We cannot sacrifice what we don't have. We have to be conscious of what we are sacrificing and in this instance, then, we must be aware of the abandoned, frozen, hidden child in ourselves, before any sacrifice can take place. This reclamation of the child is no easy task. She resides in a hidden place (like the scullery) and will emerge only after a long period during which her "adult" caretaker sniffs and scans to determine the reliability of the territory. It is here that the analyst and soul both experience the "coming and going" motif as the wounded one assesses her safety. To come to life, to enter the world of time out of the frozen timelessness that has endured for many years, there must be trust of one's own adult caretaking self and also in the integrity of the accompanying other. If these variables remain constant, the child will emerge, grieve her losses, begin to play, and ultimately decide that this world is interesting and that she wants a place in it. What emerges then from the woman is often a beautiful, thorough, and expressive emotional life, for it is the emotional life that has been frozen with the physical threat or psychologically inappropriate bonding. As tears dissolve the ice that has encased her soul, all the other emotions that have been locked in with the grieving ones also emerge: wonder, joy, pleasure in relationship, and a connectedness to herself that creates her availability to others and to the awesome religious quality of the universe.

REFERENCES

Grimm Brothers. 1960. *The Grimms' German Folk Tales.* Francis P. Magoun, Jr. and Alexander H. Krappe, trans. Carbondale, Ill.: Southern Illinois University Press.

Jung, C. G. 1952. *Symbols of Transformation*. In *Collected Works*, vol. 5. Princeton, N.J.: Princeton University Press, 1956.

Jung, C. G. 1954. Transformation symbolism in the mass. *CW* 11:201–296. Princeton, N.J.: Princeton University Press, 1958.

Plath, Sylvia. 1961. "Daddy." In *Ariel*. New York: Harper and Row, pp. 49–51.

"Beauty and the Beast" and "The Wonderful Sheep" The Couple in Fairy Tales: When Father's Daughter Meets Mother's Son

Irene Gad

For decades our therapeutic attention to the couple has been caught in the polarity of individual dynamics at one end and family/social issues at the other. Whether the focus was very wide or very narrow, this polarity has limited the range of possibilities in couple therapy when its special dynamics were made to fit either one or the other pole, i.e., reduced to the individual approach or expanded to the family system. Only sex therapists seem to center exclusively on the couple. Even so, these three focal areas are restrictive and minimize the contribution of factors that might facilitate and deepen the experience of a committed, intimate attachment within the dyad (Scarf 1987, p. 7). Above all, these approaches miss the inspiring perspective offered by Corbett:

> The body may be one sex but the soul must always carry both principles. . . . because of the intrinsic impossibility of complete incarnation of the Self into a one-sex body, the demand for relationships is inexorable, because the Self can be experienced more fully between two people. (Corbett 1990, pp. 159–160)

We bring into our coupling all our dreams and hopes, all the yearnings and the frustrations accumulated in our long-lost and ever-present childhood. An intimate attachment often reactivates old wounds received in the primary mother–child relationship. Provided the right amount of restructuring and healing has occurred at the individual level, it seems only natural to expect that what has been disrupted in the first intimate relationship may be helpfully modified by a subsequent intimate relationship with a loving partner.

In analytical psychology, fairy tales are symbolic representations of human problems and of possible solutions to these problems. Thus far, fairy tales have been interpreted mostly at the subjective level, from the point of view of either the feminine or masculine hero. Their interpretation from the couple's vantage point, however, seems justified (Kast 1983). Indeed, fairy tales may be the best possible expression of the universal need for renewal and redemption and therefore are eminently well suited to clarify deep issues in human relationships, particularly in the way men and women behave toward each other (Hart 1973, Kast 1983).

I have chosen the well-known "Beauty and the Beast" and a less familiar fairy tale, "The Wonderful Sheep," for comparison (Lang 1968). They are nearly identical except for the ending. This approach enabled me to focus on the ways the partners interacted, what determined their reaction to each other, and what factors seemed to facilitate or hinder their relationship. If our inner maps determine in part our outer landscapes, then by finding out what psychic barriers interfere with the creation of a good relationship, we may diminish the power of destructive patterns to which we so often unwillingly fall victim. By this approach I mean to discover the personal and archetypal aspects involved in the destructive or facilitating interpersonal and/or intrapersonal reactions. I attempt to identify traps the partners are bound to fall into and some mistakes that can be avoided.

The Wonderful Sheep

A king had three daughters fair and virtuous, however, the youngest was the most beautiful and he loved her the most. Her name was Marvelous. The king went to war and, returning victorious, they celebrated their reunion with a feast. After it was over, the king inquired what dream his daughters may have had prior to his return. The oldest daughter reported she had dreamed the king had given her a golden dress, the next one said she had received a golden spindle from him in her dream. Marvelous had seen herself at her second sister's wedding. In her dream, the king was holding a golden ewer and was asking permission to wash her hands. For the king, this meant enslavement and humiliation. Retaliating in his rage, he ordered his captain of the guard to take Marvelous to the forest, kill her, and bring back her tongue and her heart.

With naive trust, Marvelous went with the captain when he came to get her. Three faithful playmates—a Mooress, a dog, and a monkey—fearing the worst followed her closely. In the middle of the forest, the captain told Marvelous what the king had ordered. Her three playmates decided then and there to kill themselves in order to provide the requested tongue and heart, thus saving Marvelous's life with their sacrifice.

Remaining alone in the forest, Marvelous searched for a way out but got more lost and scared. She was becoming desperate when suddenly she heard a bleating of sheep. Going toward the clearing where the sound seemed to come from, she came upon a most wonderful sheep adorned with gold and pearls and resting under a golden canopy. He offered to help her and took her to an immense cavern. After a long descent, they arrived in a magical meadow full of the most wonderful things to eat, smell, and see.

Surrounded by bounty and beauty, they spent pleasant days with each other and the wonderful sheep fell in love with Marvelous. He decided to tell her his sad story. He had been a carefree king, feasting and hunting. One day, while chasing a stag, he saw the deer jump in a lake. As he raced after it, he fell into an abyss beneath the lake with a blazing fire at its bottom. He believed he was about to perish when he saw an old fairy whose ugliness had scared him since childhood. She was going to rescue him only if he would respond to her passionate love. Repulsed, he rejected her and was instantly changed into a sheep as were all his subjects.

A while after this, they heard that Marvelous's oldest sister was getting married. Marvelous's wish to attend was granted and she went to the wedding with the richest retinue the wonderful sheep could provide, but she had to promise to return forthwith. She took care to leave the ceremony even before it was over to keep her promise. Meanwhile the king, her father, intrigued by the fascinating unknown princess and chagrined to see her vanish, decided to prevent her from leaving should she ever return.

When news of her second sister's wedding reached them, Marvelous asked again permission to go. Despite his forebodings the wonderful sheep again gave her a lavish entourage, reminding her to return with all speed because without her he would die. This time Marvelous could not leave the church because the king, her father, had bolted all doors. The king then came, took her by the hand, and as they entered the palace, asked her to be allowed to wash her hands with his golden ewer. Overcome, Marvelous fell at his feet and reminded him of her dream. The king rejoiced upon being reunited with his beloved daughter and did all in his power to please her. Surrounded by adulation, Marvelous became oblivious of the passage of time and of her promise to the wonderful sheep.

Tortured by her absence, the wonderful sheep decided to follow her and attempt to bring her back. But her father had given strict orders to prevent anyone from reaching her. Brokenhearted, the wonderful sheep expired on the palace doorsteps where Marvelous found him as she was about to go for her daily ride with her father.

The Beauty and the Beast

A rich merchant had three daughters. The two oldest were vain, selfish, and jealous of the youngest, Beauty, who was not only beautiful but modest, charming, and helpful to everyone. The merchant, having suddenly lost all his wealth, decided to go away in an attempt to regain some of his fortune. The two oldest sisters demanded that he return with expensive presents for them; Beauty modestly asked her father only for a rose.

Returning from his unsuccessful venture, he got lost in a forest. He feared he would perish when he came upon a palace where he found food and shelter but no one about. The next morning as he was leaving, the merchant saw some beautiful roses and picked one for Beauty, remembering her request. As he did so, a hideous beast appeared and told him he will have to die for having stolen the rose. The merchant, pleading for his life, explained that he took the rose for one of his daughters. The frightful beast agreed to let him go if he sent one of his daughters to take his place. If none of his daughters was willing to come, the merchant had to return within three months. Upon having agreed, the merchant received from the beast a chest full of gold.

When he reached home, the merchant gave Beauty her rose but could not help telling her what had happened. Beauty returned with her father to the palace, and the beast, making sure she had come to him of her own free will, asked the father to leave.

From then on the beast wooed Beauty and met all her wishes. She grew accustomed to his hideous shape as his kindness and gentleness moved her. But whenever he asked her to marry him, as he often did, she would only refuse, much to his distress.

One day, while looking in a magic mirror, she saw her ailing father pining away for her and asked permission to go home to reassure him. The beast gave her a week's time to do so, but warned her he would die if she failed to return. At home the envious sisters plotted to detain Beauty beyond the week in the hope that the monstrous beast would destroy her in his fury. Beauty allowed herself to be persuaded, but during the tenth night she saw the beast in a dream, reproaching her in a dying voice. She wished herself back and found the beast near death. Overwhelmed with grief, Beauty kissed him and promised to marry him.

At this, the beast turned into a handsome prince. He had been under the spell of a wicked witch and had to remain in a beastly shape until a beautiful girl loved him enough to marry him. They were joined for the wedding by her father while her evil sisters, now turned into stone, had to witness her happiness and remain in that state until they were able to own up to their faults.

Generally, it is accepted in fairy-tale interpretation that each character represents an aspect of the hero or heroine. For instance, when the father gives the order to have the heroine killed, it means that the father complex is the basis of her animus possession and that she is in the grips of this destructive animus. A more recent approach would take the situation depicted in the fairy tale and make the attempt to describe what it feels like to find oneself in a similar predicament (Asper-Bruggisser 1986). This way of "entering" experientially into a fairy tale facilitates the use of fairy-tale interpretation in therapy. As often happens, the situation an analysand is in reminds us of a fairy-tale image (Kast 1982). For instance, a talented young woman hiding her creative spirit behind a drab exterior because of an unloving, critical mother may remind us of Cinderella. Should the analyst narrate the story, the analysand will be able to identify with the fairy-tale image without all the resistances that a therapeutic interpretation may mobilize. Moreover, this identification will allow healing through an emotional/experiential recognition and will avoid a purely intellectual understanding that is therapeutically much less effective.

The two fairy tales show a father's daughter meeting a mother's son. I will attempt to compare the way the puella/father's daughter interacts with the puer/mother's son in both.

THE PUER/FATHER

Our two fairy tales share the same motif presented in the Italian folk tale "Bene come il sale," in a Romanian tale "Sarea'n bucate," in a German tale "Die Gänsehirtin am Brunnen," and in the English folk tale "Rushcap," made famous by Shakespeare in his *King Lear.* It is the story of the beloved third daughter rejected by the father because of the way she expresses her love for him. In *King Lear*, the king feels this expression of love to be inadequate and incomprehensible; in "The Wonderful Sheep," the king feels threatened and humiliated by it. Kirsch (1966), in his analysis of *King Lear*, argues that Shakespeare has used this motif in order to make Lear appear childish, demanding from his daughter the completely dedicated love a mother has for her child. If he can't have what he wants from Cordelia, he doesn't want her at all and banishes her in a blinding rage. Kirsch argues that Lear has projected his anima upon Cordelia: according to his image of her, she should have spoken words of praise and love. However, her words plunge him into an abyss, because, when delivered, his anima projections are instantly destroyed. Lear has yet to understand that:

> The beloved is not only a mirror in which we can find ourselves; through love, we envision the best possibilities in the beloved and give that person the feeling that those possibilities can be realized. When we truly love, we will also forgive the beloved if those possibilities are not completely realized. (Kast 1986, p. 5)

Hillman (1979) points out that behind the father/senex one finds the puer, the senex/puer being the two poles of the same archetype. This not only confirms Kirsch's analysis of Lear but can also explain the devastating effect a puer/father can have on his daughter's development (Leonard 1978). When the daughter becomes the father's anima carrier, this can create in the daughter a lack of confidence in her own nature which will then make it difficult for her to reach a sense of wholeness and inner harmony. by identifying with her father's anima, she will be separated from her own feminine self. Her true femininity will remain undeveloped, and the maturation of her personality will be prevented. This stunting will occur whether the relationship with the father is one of intense love or hate (von Beit 1975).

THE PUER/FATHER'S DAUGHTER

Being the first man in her life, the father will constellate for the daughter the image of masculinity, he will build a bridge toward her future partner. If, however, he should want to keep her to himself, he may destroy the foundation in which her womanhood is rooted. An excessive attachment to her father will make a woman dedicate herself, perhaps for life, to the impersonal intellectual, and/or the utopic abstract (Allenby 1955).

A negative father may make his daughter feel insecure by giving her the message that she is uninteresting to a man. By his attitude, he can imply she is not a valid opponent in an intellectual debate and may even be inadequate as a sex partner or as a life companion. Consequently, the father's daughter may suffer from insecurity, instability, lack of self-confidence, anxiety, and in general, a weak ego (Leonard 1977). She becomes a puella praised for her compliance, adaptability, gentleness, youthful sweetness, and obedient cooperation.

We can recognize these qualities in Marvelous. She meekly follows the captain of the guard and willingly accepts the death of her three playmates. The Mooress, whose swarthy complexion may depict the darker side of Marvelous, could stand for her instinctual, primitive, chthonic tendencies. The dog may represent her sexuality and fertility. The monkey – both wise and foolish – symbolizes, according to Hillman, partly the "polymorphous perversity" of the pleasure principle and partly the guardian angel (1979, p. 45). Their death may illustrate the sacrifice of her feminine instincts in order to buy her way back into the kingdom of her father with her compliance.

We can speculate on the hidden relationship between Grimm's Snow White and Marvelous, both condemned to be killed in the forest. The direct order is given by the witch-stepmother to the hunter for Snow White and by the king to the captain for Marvelous. This suggests that Marvelous also has a witch somewhere in the background, constellated by the absence of the queen mother.

If one compares the captain with the hunter and looks also at other interpretations (von Beit 1975, p. 706) one could say that the captain may be regarded as an animus figure pushed into a destructive role by the dominant collective consciousness represented by the king whose servant he is.

It is the hunter in "Snow White" who is sent to kill the heroine. The hunter's profession is closely connected with animals. His pity for Snow White and sparing of her life can be interpreted as:

> a healthy instinct or natural attitude (which) enables one to preserve positive emotions from the onslaught of evil. Sometimes people simply have enough instinct to protect themselves, or their better side, from the attacks of the dark. (Birkhauser-Oeri 1988, p. 35)

By contrast the lack of inner source of instinctive nourishment makes Marvelous vulnerable to be swept away through the underworld cavern into the magic meadows of the wonderful sheep. This quality of unrealness is encountered in Lewis's version of "Amor and Psyche" (1956) and in the "ghostlike unreality of Psyche's paradise" as Neumann calls it (1973b, p. 73). This has been repeatedly my experience with some of my "father's daughter" analysands. They had an inordinate capacity to create for themselves an enchanted, unrealistic world. Their naive dedication to the most lofty ideals was paralleled by an almost total lack of awareness of the darkness in their partner or in themselves.

Children are influenced by their parents consciously and unconsciously, especially when the parent has an unresolved problem. What is unresolved in the parent becomes the child's burden. And fairy tales depict this situation, e.g., being sold to the devil or a witch. In "The Handless Maiden," the heroine is sold to the devil by her father.

> A woman with such a father has not been nourished . . . a destructive devilish intellectualism, a deadly animus, will take possession of her or a power drive, and she will become as cold, ruthless and brutal as her father was. (von Franz 1976, pp. 76–79)

At times a rebellious daughter may reject her puer/father by consciously taking an extreme senex stance, only to be confronted with the denied puer aspect when it constellates in her unconscious (Leonard 1982, p. 17). This image of the masculine splits into its opposites: weak youth/sadistic old man. We find its expression in Marvelous's story when she encounters the sadistic old man in her father and the weak youth in the wonderful sheep.

It has been stated that in retaliation the daughter with a father complex will seek to mortify a powerful father by taking on inferior lovers (Carducci 1983, p. 48). Furthermore, at another level, a weak partner enables her to maintain admiration of the idealized father exclusively. Finally her choice of a weak partner fulfills a wish to dedicate herself to someone who, unbeknownst to her, is similar to her father, thus she will fall for a puer in search of a mother/bride.

THE MOTHER'S SON

"The Wonderful Sheep" depicts our hero hunting in the forest and following a deer. The deer represents an unconscious factor that acts as a guide to consciousness (von Franz 1951). According to Kast, the deer has the task to lure the hero to the beyond (Jacoby, Kast, and Riedel 1978, p. 116). It can embody those captivating ideas, fascinating feelings, elusive inklings that one cannot grasp but that may finally lead to the complex. In the fairy tale the deer jumps into a lake; the hero follows and falls into water, symbol of the unconscious. There, according to Jung, "the treasure hard to obtain" lies hidden and only the brave will be able to reach it (1944, par. 155). But our hero falls beyond the bottom of the lake into an abyss filled with blazing fire. Here he meets the old witch who attempts to seduce him, but when rejected, turns him into a sheep. This image evokes the picture of a childish psyche in which the fiery passions of instinctual forces, represented by the witch, have generated a defensive regression (Ulanov and Ulanov 1985). Regression of the libido will

> reactivate the ways and habits of childhood, and above all the relation to the mother; but what was natural and useful to the child is a psychic danger for the adult . . . the infantile attachment is a crippling limitation. (Jung 1952, par. 313)

We know nothing about the wonderful sheep's parents. He mentions only the witch and her devouring passion. In the absence of a father, we would expect our hero to have difficulties with his role identification, as well as with his masculine development in general. Indeed, we have to confront the father imago if we are to avoid remaining forever in bondage to its rule. A father is particularly important to a son because the son will feel stronger in his masculine role when he can have a direct model of what it means to be a man, a husband, a family head, and a father. The father's presence will instill in the son

> a modicum of self-possession and self-assertion – distilled . . . out of mutual sameness or shared maleness – which renders the wider world not only manageable and conquerable but infinitely alluring. (Blos 1985, p. 11)

In the absence of a queen mother, we would expect, as for Marvelous, that the mother archetype will constellate in its negative aspects. It was therefore not surprising that we encountered the devouring witch. We can easily see the similarities between this fairy-tale figure and the mythological image of the Great Goddess, passionate and demanding. When thwarted, she will take revenge by making the hero/reluctant lover mad, impotent, or even by killing him. Whether we call her witch or Great Goddess, the result of her vindictiveness is always the overpowering of the ego (Neumann 1973a, pp. 90–93).

The witch personifies for Ulanov an archetypal force luring us from our familiar world into her far country remote from human concerns – in fairy-tale language, either dark forests or deep lakes. She can activate connections to primordial forces at the edge of being, where, if we can face the fear of the unknown she represents, we may be unexpectedly renewed. Yet from her remote habitation, beyond the reach of reason, she may exert her fearful power upon us; she may invade consciousness and possess it.

> A witch's spell exerts this anesthetizing effect on our consciousness . . . we are put to sleep . . . we lose our voice . . . we are reduced to beastly form . . . we are fixed to one spot . . . we turn to stone. (Ulanov 1977, pp. 7–8)

When domination of the unconscious – the mother – prevents the development of the son trapped in the unconscious, he appears in fairy tales as the hybrid monster caught in an animal stage of development (von Beit 1975, p. 4). Jung has said that

> insofar as one is possessed by the mood of a certain animal or plant . . . one *is* it and one loses one's identity. (1976, p. 465)

The emotional character of the hero will be expressed by the animal shape he will assume. For instance, a sensitive and easily hurt person, who out of defensiveness is also very wounding to others, will be represented in fairy tales by a hedgehog, as in Grimm's "Hans My Hedgehog."

The sheep is an animal who is traditionally associated with gloom, melancholy, and depression (Hillman 1971, p. 109). White and innocent, it is a symbol of simplicity and gentleness (Matthews 1986). When we compare the sheep to the other animals used as suitors in the known variants of the tale – the lion, bear, squirrel, raven, pig, frog – we are struck by the emasculated weakness and meekness of the sheep (Thompson 1955). In reality we are dealing with a passive – aggressive character, illustrated by two contrasting symbols closely associated with the sheep: the sacrificial lamb, symbol of Christ, and the ram, symbol of destructive male aggressivity (Neumann 1973b). The lamb allegories of early Christian art represent, in Jung's view, not only the lofty love of God but also sentimentality and infantilism (Jung 1952, par. 667).

In the ram, we may see the repressed shadow of the sheep in our fairy tale. The effect shadow repression can have is made quite vivid by two passages from *The Vision Seminars*:

> People who do not possess and are not aware of their inferior shadow side, may appear to be marvelously good people. . . . They tell you themselves that nothing is wrong with them; every one else is wrong, but never they . . . they are as white as milk. . . . Yet, because they deny their shadow, such people are absolutely possessed by devils. (Jung 1976, pp. 211–213)

When not possessed by devils, the lamblike innocent will attract upon himself devilish fury from the people around him (Hillman 1979, p. 112). Even so, by his very weakness and fragility, the sheepish puer can dominate through the power of his neediness. He may constellate the nurse. Yet with the milk may come the Great Mother who gags with too much giving or, worse, devours, poisons, and destroys (ibid.).

-y tales, the queen mother is not mentioned. Indeed, as -pressed in the shape of our heroes and by the activities of our heroines, this initial situation has different effects. Contrast the naive and guileless sheep – symbol of helplessness and patience (Matthews 1986) – with the hideous and scary beast – symbol of sadistic and destructive forces (Read 1961). Each seems to express what the other one hides, as though they are shadow figures for each other. While the beast hides his kindness and caring by displaying his ugly side, the wonderful sheep is apparently all gentleness without any sign of aggressivity or even assertiveness.

Given the outcome of the two fairy tales, it would seem that redemption is easier when the shadow is acknowledged, as in the beast, rather than when it is repressed, as in the wonderful sheep. As Jung reminds us,

> our shadow really exists. It is as evil as we are positive and constructive in consciousness . . . the more desperately we try to be good and wonderful and perfect, the more the shadow develops a definite will to be black and evil and destructive. People cannot see that; they are always striving to be marvelous, then they discover terrible destructive things happening which they cannot understand. . . . The fact is that if one tries beyond one's capacity to be perfect, the shadow descends to hell and becomes the devil. For it is just as sinful from the standpoint of nature and of truth to be above oneself as to be below oneself. (1976, p. 213)

The nonviolent sheep is a model of overidentification with one's civilized side that leads, according to Wheelwright (1980), to an explosive situation. I have worked with a couple where the most violent outbursts of the wife were invariably triggered by her husband's retreat behind a placating attitude. Under the guise of an amiable, peace-loving person, he was hiding an incapacity to confront the destructive aggressivity of her animus.

For Marvelous, who like the wonderful sheep has no shadow, the sisters are just a fortuitous occasion to return to the world of the father. The sisters are evident shadow figures, actively hostile and envious, in the case of Beauty and in "Amor and Psyche." Could it be that the shadow may help against the destructive effects of a negative parent? Marvelous may be unconsciously bitter and resentful toward her father after being so brutally rejected, having sacrificed her "companions" to make herself more acceptable, but to no avail. These negative feelings are repressed by Marvelous but in "Amor and Psyche" the hostility toward the masculine is evident in the sisters' advice to Psyche. They suggest she cut off her lover's head: an ancient symbol of castration, sublimated in the spiritual sphere. The man's murder and castration are, according to Neumann, matriarchal symbols of self-defense and/or domination (1973b, p. 72). The modern father's daughter refuses to be the victim of the man or king she once adored. But, because she still does not recognize her own demonic side, she projects it onto the masculine world and seeks revenge for what she perceives to be the murder of her femininity. Bewitched by her own power drive and cut off from her chthonic femininity, she fails to recognize in her revenge a disguised form of suicide. Warped and unconnected, her femininity is neither rediscovered nor redeemed. It is by accepting not only her very human helplessness, but also her capacity for evil as well as good, that she will be open to redemption and will be able to integrate her animus (Woodman 1980).

The beast seems to know that the only way out is to give up any ambivalence that makes the yearned-for human shape half desired, half feared. However agonizing the pain, he knows he must abandon the protective darkness of his animal shape if he is to succeed. He seems to have understood that salvation does not come from either running away or from drifting (Jung 1944, par. 200). This is illustrated in our fairy tales by the fact that the beast has a palace in the forest, while the wonderful sheep only makes believe he has a place of his own. He is the one drifting and giving in. His kind of apathy was described by Neumann as a complete impotence against the uroboric Mother and the overwhelming fate she meted out:

> Masculinity and consciousness have not yet won independence . . . the death ecstasy is symptomatic . . . the doomed and sorrowful hero succumbs to the Great Mother. (1973a, p. 88)

He succumbs without a struggle to that inertia that has to be given up since the dawn of time in order to avoid annihilation (von Beit 1975, p. 220). And, as we have seen, he is annihilated.

According to Walder (1956), the relationship between mother and son may retain into adulthood the character of a partial identity, a *participation mystique*. The result is an inability to love, and resistance to loving, in turn, produces regression (Jung 1952, pars. 253–2524). However, the puer/son also seeks relationships that could give meaning to his existence, that could provide him with

> the kind of reflection he is unable to perform for himself. . . . In effect the puer does not relate to object (in an analytic sense), he relates instead to the missing part of himself. (Satinover 1980, p. 96)

But it is not by forcing his partner to incarnate his missing aspects; rather, it is through a real intimate relationship with his mate that the puer has any chance to heal his soul. Unfortunately, victim of his negative mother complex, he will be unable to commit himself.

While the animal/prince is under a spell that keeps him in bondage to a dark witch/mother figure who will not let him go free, the bewitched princess is in thrall to a demonic father figure. Just as fear of the Great Mother can express itself in a man by a refusal to love and to commit himself, a father fixation may result in an incapacity of the woman to enter into a real relationship. In fairy tales this is usually expressed by the heroine refusing the suitors or even having them killed if they don't answer her riddles. In "The Wonderful Sheep," the lack of love is expressed by Marvelous failing to return, a forgetfulness showing her lack of involvement. While Beauty is kept from returning by the masked animosity of her sisters, Marvelous's return is prevented by her father's disguised seductiveness.

> The animus can devalue and falsify a relationship with its evil interference; whenever a woman lets herself be dominated by it she may find herself pushed against her will in a direction imposed by forces she is unable to withstand. (von Beit 1975, p. 743)

The king's order to close the doors to prevent Marvelous from leaving represents just such an interference. The result is the break of the relationship to the wonderful sheep.

Because the two aspects of the puer/senex archetype are not integrated in her father, the puella is "bewitched" by his unconscious. The father himself being a puer turns his anima projection onto his daughter and she thus becomes his inspiration, his "child-bride." She may remain faithful for the rest of her life to this "husband," fixated in an Electra complex, unless she recognizes that her father/lover is in reality the image of her own inner ideal male, who must not be projected upon a human man. For she may spend her life searching for this ideal. Jung describes this type of woman thus:

> It is all up with the man whom the whims of fortune bring into contact with this infantile woman: he will at once be made identical with her animus-hero and relentlessly set up as the ideal figure, threatened with the direst punishments should he ever make a face that shows the slightest departure from the ideal. (1952, par. 465)

Marvelous is not the friendly female assisting the hero to free himself from the spell of the devouring mother. She seems to lack the

> sisterly side of woman, standing shoulder to shoulder with the hero as his beloved, helpmate and companion or as the Eternal Feminine who leads him to redemption . . . touchingly ready to sacrifice themselves and to love him with their purely human love whose very difference complement our own. (Neumann 1973a, p. 201)

Beauty seems to have reached that understanding. She also seems aware that

> where one is weak one needs support and completion . . . (and that) in fact, a woman's place is on the weak side of man. (Jung 1948, par. 440)

Marvelous, by contrast, has nothing to offer to her mate.

The great misfortune of this father's daughter is that her own mother has usually failed her. She blames herself for feeling unlovable, and being unloved becomes synonymous with being abnormal or bad. When the primal relationship is negative, the instinct of self-preservation prematurely gives rise to a negativized ego which will use defense mechanisms to substitute for the love, acceptance, and security the negative mother failed to provide (Neumann 1976).

Having never developed a connection to her own nature, the father's daughter simply does not comprehend the feminine principle. For her, being receptive means surrendering control, opening herself to a fate she has not learned to trust and plummeting through chaotic darkness into an abyss that has no bottom. Convinced no loving arms will open to receive her as she falls, she dares not surrender to life.

The fear of the feminine abyss is a reality for women with a negative mother complex. Flight into the world of the fathers is a characteristic response to it. But there comes a time when the gods of the patriarchy, to which the woman has dedicated sometimes her entire life, no longer respond. Life for such a woman loses its meaning (Perera 1981). That is when she has to go back to the painful and terrifying realm of the Mothers in order to reconnect with those qualities Psyche had never lost: relatedness, receptivity, patience, tenderness, tenacious, firm, and flexible love (Neumann 1973b).

Father's daughters will look for the mother they never had in their partners and they will be attracted by mother's sons because of their "feminine" qualities. They are yearning for the warmth and support they were never given and thus were never able to develop in themselves. Unfortunately, although the puers are in touch with the unconscious and its creative depths, they have no connection to the chthonic aspect of the feminine archetype that could have brought them down to earth.

Our fairy-tale couples, Marvelous and the wonderful sheep, and Beauty and the beast, are both in the forest, that place where "things begin to turn and grow again . . . a healing regression" (von Franz 1976, p. 85). This time in the forest is time for transformation in a *temenos* where renewal can occur. Cut off from the everyday world, they may come in contact with the forces of nature and the unknown or with repressed forces within themselves. This time can be looked upon as representing those periods in which a major loss has plunged us into despair and is forcing us to reconsider our entire life.

What would be needed now is the capacity to endure, but this a puer's daughter cannot have because

> by disposition he (her father) has not developed the quality to hold, to bear through a difficult situation. . . . Even where senex emphasis is in the foreground . . . puerile moods and impulses are in the unconscious, popping out irrationally at unexpected moments. (Leonard 1977)

We have no difficulty seeing Marvelous's father fit into this picture. With this kind of model, it is not surprising that she seems constantly to be coming and going instead of staying "in the forest," with the process. In contrast to Marvelous and despite the attempts to keep her away, Beauty remembers the beast and returns to him, later than promised but nevertheless in time to save his life and the relationship.

Time in the forest of despair, time of opportunity to contact inner strength and inner truth, may be wasted because opportunity to change does not mean that change will occur. Beauty has the courage to face this challenge and change but Marvelous has not. Beauty comes out of the forest and goes to her father's house following an inner movement. She has been nurtured by the kindness and care she has received and she now has the capability to be concerned about another's well being. She sees her father is ailing and this is why she wants to go to him. In contrast, Marvelous wants to go to her sisters' weddings as a distraction, a collective outer event without any redeeming quality for the soul. It reminds me of some analysands who use certain outer events to reemerge prematurely from their inner journey and who restructure their life along an incompletely achieved self-awareness. It never works.

The fairy tales also show that lost parts of ourselves may be mediated by a partner upon whom these unacknowledged parts can be projected. This opportunity to recognize and reclaim that which we now clearly see, because we face it in the other, is most challenging. However, more often than not, the fear of change is such that rather than accept the challenge and the change, we give up and run away from ourself and our partner, a mirror we are too scared to look into. Thus implicitly, we give up also on the relationship.

While Beauty and the beast are able to change, Marvelous and the wonderful sheep fail; she returns to her father and he dies. It seems to me that the wonderful sheep's death can represent the end result of a relationship dynamic described by Satinover (1980, p. 101). He observes that in the puer/puella relationship beneath the anima/animus projection, one also finds the projection of the childhood Self. When the relationship fails, there is not only reactivation of the narcissistic wounding but also a shattering of identity.

Beauty can redeem the beast because she observes and appreciates his kindness and comes to love him. She is sensitive to him, feels his need and his distress, dreams of him, and returns to him. Marvelous receives all the gifts and the attention the wonderful sheep bestows upon her, but we have no sense that these are appreciated by her. Her lack of appreciation may express the incapacity of the "emotionally autistic" narcissist to receive, use, and be nourished by what is given, thus remaining perpetually hungry.

I believe that we can talk about narcissistic wounding in connection with the couple, Marvelous and the wonderful sheep. The nonacceptance of their shadow, the repression of their aggressivity, the sheep's inertia as well as Marvelous's impatience and incapacity for giving or receiving, are all traits described as characteristic of the narcissistically wounded in the various works of Balint, Guex, Miller, Kohut, Neumann, Schwartz-Salant, Winnicott, and others.*

Because of the particular sensitivity narcissistically wounded people have developed in interaction with their first "love object," they have learned to sense what their loved one expects them to be like. Unfortunately, behind the mask they have learned to put on, they remain unrecognized and therefore unloved and unnourished. Their wound has little chance to heal under these circumstances. Moreover, the expectations they have forged in imitation of and/or in contrast to the parental imago will form the image of an ideal partner that will build an unconscious barrier to the interaction with the real partner.

Tragically, those most crippled emotionally are also the most helpless and needy. Their narcissistic wounds make them the most hungry and dependent for warm and constant affection and for an acceptance they never had. They will seek to still this yearning in an intimate relationship. However, their hunger and yearning becomes a tantalic torture. On one hand, this mounting intensity cannot be stilled by a partner who is merely human and fallible. On the other hand, the emotional autism produced by

---

*M. Balint, *The Basic Fault* (New York: Brunner-Mazel, 1979); J. Bowlby, *The Making and Breaking of Affectional Bonds* (London: Tavistock, 1979); G. Guex, *La nevrose d'abandon* (Paris: PUF, 1960); H. Kohut, *The Analysis of the Self* (New York: International Universities Press, 1971) and *The Restoration of the Self* (New York: International Universities Press, 1977); M. Mahler, F. Pine, and A. Bergman, *The Psychological Birth of the Human Infant* (London: Maresfeld Library, 1975); A. Miller, *Prisoners of Childhood* (New York: Basic Books, 1979); E. Neumann, *The Child* (New York: Harper Colophon Books, 1976); N. Schwartz-Salant, *Narcissism and Character Transformation* (Toronto: Inner City Books, 1982); D. W. Winnicott, *Playing and Reality* (London: Tavistock, 1971).

their narcissistic wound makes it impossible for them to accept the very love they long for, even if they encounter a partner willing to nurture them.

CONCLUSION

As long as the partners in a couple remain bound to their father and/or mother complex, the couple will not and cannot survive. Commitment to a partner can never really be negotiated by two autistic emotional cripples caught in the inner prison of a negative mother and father. The couple can be a source of satisfaction and growth only when vulnerability can be shared. The courage to do so is available only to those individuals who have dared to descend into the darkness of their own souls and have risked the painful "night sea journey." Ultimately, it is our inner stance toward pain that will transform its experience into growth. If pain is "nothing but" an unpleasant event to be avoided at all cost, by all manner of defense mechanisms – blaming, avoidance, projection, or denial – then nothing will be gained.

Unable to cope with pain and intimacy, the narcissistically wounded enter a round of relationships with big hopes only to see them dissolve in despair. This will only confirm the initial unconscious premise that life is as bad as one's other was and that one will never find the "one and only" with whom one can enter paradise.

Passive resignation and hopeless isolation used to be the way out when one felt unable to cope with, or invest in, one's partner. Today, active breaking up of the couple is the way. This is often associated with a regressive return to mother. What usually follows, however, is projection of one's fantasies onto the next partner. This behavior is dictated by incapacity to see gratification delayed, by intolerance for failure, and by impatience. The deeper the narcissistic wound, the sooner hopelessness and despair set in. As if cursed and spellbound, the partners in a narcissistic couple feel they will never be understood or nurtured. They also find out that the temporary and illusory moments of happiness gained at the price of "selling one's soul" are paid not in a beyond very few believe in anymore, but in a future nearer than they had realized.

The tragic wound that forces a child to become a premature pseudo-adult will, paradoxically, keep the crippled child alive, behind the unbreachable walls of its own defensive fortress. Perhaps they will marry, yet no eternal puer/son can be a husband and no eternal puella/daughter can be a wife. Should they procreate, neither will be a "good enough" parent to their children. Thus the "sins" of the parents will be cast upon their children. Or, in fairy-tale language, the children will be bewitched or sold to the devil.

Fairy tales teach us that curses can be lifted. What is needed is a capacity to love, a willingness for sacrifice, and a patient acceptance of the inevitable pain. This purposeful perseverance and dedication will make way for the necessary transformation.

These are the very qualities narcissistically wounded people do not have.

With luck, we receive some fateful warning and we heed it. When Beauty came close to losing the beast, she then realized how much he meant to her. When she gives him the redeeming kiss and promises to marry him, the curse is lifted. The beast is transformed into a prince.

Here, at the end, Zimmer's words ring out:

> the curse is lifted because the unconscious is transformed, *change and you will step into a changed world!* (1938, p. 231; author's translation)

REFERENCES

Allenby, A. I. 1955. The father archetype in feminine psychology. *Journal of Analytical Psychology* 1:79–92.

Asper-Bruggisser, K. 1986. Der therapeutische umgang mit schattenaspekten der narzissitischen stoerung. *Analytishe Psychologie* 17:1-24.

Birkhauser-Oeri, S. 1988. *The Mother: Archetypal Image in Fairy Tales*. Toronto: Inner City Books.

Blos, P. 1985. *Son and Father*. New York: Free Press.

Carducci, P. 1983. Bene come il sale. Diploma thesis. Zurich: C. G. Jung Institute.

Corbett, L. 1990. The archetypal feminine: a response to Betty Meador, "Forward into the Past." In *Dreams in Analysis*, N. Schwartz-Salant and M. Stein, eds. Wilmette, Ill.: Chiron Publications.

Grimm, the Brothers. 1987. *The Complete Fairy Tales of the Brothers Grimm*. New York: Bantam.

Hart, D. L. 1973. Classic man–woman models in fairytales. *Quadrant* 13:12–17.

Hillman, J. 1971. The feeling function. In *Jung's Typology*, von Franz and Hillman, eds. Zurich: Spring Publications, pp. 75–150.

_____. 1979. *Puer Papers*. Dallas: Spring Publications.

Jacoby, J., Kast, V., and Riedel, I. 1978. *Das Böse im Märchen*. Fellbach: Bonz.

Jung, C. G. 1944. *Psychology and Alchemy. CW*, vol. 12. London: Routledge and Kegan, 1970.

_____. 1948. The phenomenology of the spirit in fairytales. *CW* 9i:207–254. Princeton, N.J.: Princeton University Press, 1980.

_____. 1952. *Symbols of Transformation. CW*, vol. 5. London: Routledge and Kegan, 1970.

_____. 1976. *The Vision Seminars*. Zurich: Spring Publications.

Kast, V. 1982. *Wege aus Angst und Symboise*. Olten: Walter.

_____. 1983. *Man und Frau im Märchen*. Olten:Walter.

_____. 1986. *The Nature of Loving*. Wilmette, Ill.: Chiron Publications.

Kirsch, J. 1966. King Lear. In *Shakespeare's Royal Self*. New York: Putnam, pp. 185–319.

Lang, A. 1968. *The Blue Fairytale Book*. New York: Dover.

Leonard, L. 1977. Puer's daughter. *Psychological Perspectives* 8/1.

_____. 1978. Puella patterns. *Psychological Perspectives* 9.

_____. 1982. *The Wounded Woman*. Chicago: Swallow Press.

Lewis, C. S. 1956. *Till We Have Faces*. New York: Harcourt, Brace, and Jovanovich.

Matthews, B., trans. 1986. *The Herder Symbol Dictionary*. Wilmette, Ill.: Chiron Publications.

Neumann, E. 1973a. *The Origins and History of Consciousness*. Princeton, N.J.: Princeton University Press.

_____. 1973b. *Amor and Psyche: The Psychic Development of the Feminine*. Princeton, N.J.: Princeton University Press.

_____. 1976. *The Child*. New York: Harper Colophon Books.

Perera, S. 1981. *Descent to the Goddess*. Toronto: Inner City Books.

Read, H. 1961. The beauty and the beast. *Eranos* 30:175–210.

Satinover, J. 1980. Puer aeternus: the narcissistic relation to the self. *Quadrant* 13:75–108.

Scarf, M. 1987. *Intimate Partners*. New York: Random House.

Thompson, S. 1955. *Motif Index of Folk Literature*. Bloomington, Ind.: Indiana University Press.

Ulanov, A. 1977. The witch archetype. *Quadrant* 10:3–22.

Ulanov, A., and Ulanov, B. 1985. *The Witch and the Clown*. Wilmette, Ill.: Chiron Publications.

von Beit, H. 1975. *Symbolik des Märchens*. Bern: Franke.

von Franz, M.-L. 1951. Archetypal patterns in fairytales. Lectures. Zurich: C. G. Jung Institute.

_____. 1976. *The Feminine in Fairytales*. New York: Spring Publications.

Walder, P. 1956. Struktur und analyse eines grenzenfals. Diploma thesis. Zurich: C. G. Jung Institute.

Wheelright, J. B. 1980. *St. George and the Dandelion*. San Francisco: C. G. Jung Institute of San Francisco.

Woodman, M. 1980. *The Owl Was a Baker's Daughter.* Toronto: Inner City Books.

Zimmer, H. 1938. *Die Weisheit Indiens: Märchen und Sinnbilder.* Darmstadt: Wittich. English translation: *The King and the Corpse* (Princeton, N.J.: Princeton University Press, 1973).

Cinderella
An Interpretation*

Anne Baring

The version of Cinderella best known today is based on the Perrault story of 1697 called *Cendrillon* and that of the Brothers Grimm of 1812.

Cinderella is the daughter of a widower who marries a woman with two daughters of her own, as proud and bad tempered as she is. Cinderella is reduced to the level of a drudge in her father's new family. She is dressed by her stepmother in rags or a grey cloak and, after her work is finished, sits by the chimney corner among the ashes of the fire, her face and hands and clothes blackened by soot.

The king's son is to give a ball and invites all the young women of the kingdom to it so that he may choose his bride from among them. Cinderella's stepsisters are invited and she helps to dress them for the ball, while they taunt her about her dirty clothes and the impossibility of her going to the ball with them. The stepmother and her daughters leave, and Cinderella sits weeping by the ashes of the fire.

*The material for this paper is based on *The Myth of the Goddess: The Evolution of an Image* by Jules Cashford and Anne Baring (forthcoming from Viking Arkana, Spring 1991).

Suddenly her fairy godmother appears, finds her crying, and says she shall go to the ball. She sends Cinderella into the garden to fetch a pumpkin, hollows it out, and, striking it with her wand, transforms it into a golden coach. Cinderella finds a trap with six white mice in it and they are changed into white horses. She suggests a rat for coachman and selects one of three she finds in a trap. It is transformed in a similar manner. Six lizards are found behind a watering pot and become footmen. Cinderella's godmother then transforms her blackened rags into a sumptuous dress of silver and gold which glitters with jewels and gives her a pair of glass slippers, warning her to leave the ball before midnight, when coach, coachman, horses, footmen, and herself will all resume their original forms.

Cinderella promises to remember the warning and sets off for the ball, where she is greeted by the prince who has been advised of the arrival of an unknown princess. Her beauty amazes everyone at the ball and the prince falls deeply in love with her and will dance with no one else. Cinderella leaves the ball before midnight and returns to her godmother, asking to go again the next night. The two sisters return and tell her of the beautiful princess who has enchanted the prince.

Again Cinderella goes to the ball in a dress more splendid than the night before. Again she leaves before midnight. On the third night, however, she leaves too late, and as she hurries away from the palace, midnight strikes. She finds her dress has once again become rags and makes her way home without coach or footmen. The prince rushes after her, but she eludes him. However, in her haste, she leaves a glass slipper on the steps of the palace and this the prince retrieves.

Questioned as to the path of her flight, the palace guards say they have seen no one save a poorly clad girl with one glass shoe. The prince declares he will only marry the girl whose foot fits the shoe he holds. He comes eventually to Cinderella's home where the stepsisters try to fit their feet into the slipper. In some versions they cut off heel and toe to squeeze their foot into it. Cinderella asks to be allowed to try, too, and the stepsisters mock her. As the slipper is placed on her foot, she draws the other from her pocket and puts it on. Her godmother appears and transforms her rags into a beautiful dress, whereupon she is recognized as the princess at the ball. Her stepsisters beg to be forgiven for the way they treated her. Cinderella forgives them and is taken to the palace for her marriage to the prince.

So runs one version of the fairy tale which never fails to enchant.

Fairy tales speak with the immemorial wisdom of the soul to provide the elements that have been ignored or devalued by the conscious cultural tradition. They tell the story of what has happened to the missing elements and what still needs to happen for the balance in archetypal imagery to be restored. They may, therefore, conceal within their symbolic language both a historical record and a prophecy. The story of Cinderella has many possible interpretations, including the modern feminist one, but Harold Bayley, in the early years of this century, was the first to see it as a story of the soul's transformation and to connect it with gnostic, Egyptian, and Sumerian myth. Included in this "story of the soul" is her bondage to a cruel stepmother, the mysteries of her transformation with the help of her "true" mother, godmother or fairy godmother, the quest of the prince to find his bride, and finally the celebration of the royal marriage. With masterly economy, the story of Cinderella reflects at the archetypal level the soul's perennial plight and need, and bears witness at a historical level to her experience during the many centuries of her sojourn in time and space. Bayley's interpretation seems to me to be one of the most relevant and interesting contributions to the questions being raised today with regard to the nature of consciousness.

At the beginning of this century, in his book *The Lost Language of Symbolism* (1912), Bayley traced the historical transmission of many different stories and symbols that centered around the image of light hidden in darkness, a light which had to be rescued, redeemed, and recovered. Through a profound knowledge of the etymology of words, and an equally profound knowledge of European paper-making and the water marks that were the medium of transmission of alchemical and gnostic ideas during an era of cruel persecution, he drew an astonishing picture of the relationship between mythology and the fairy tales that found their way into many different centers of European culture. Some 345 versions of the story of Cinderella from all over the world were gathered together and published by the Folklore Society some time before he started his book, and he drew on a wealth of material from these to show the relationship between Sumero-Babylonian mythology, the Song of Songs (Song of Solomon), gnostic imagery, and this fairy tale (Cox 1893). The interpretation that follows is grounded on his associations.

Cinderella personifies both the exiled human soul, cut off from Paradise and her Mother and Father in heaven, and also the "light" of the Holy Spirit of Wisdom which is hidden within the soul, unsought and unrecognized until events are set in motion by the appeal to her "God"-mother. The story of Cinderella reveals the outlines of the great Bronze Age lunar myth of the sacred marriage between the goddess and her son-consort, transmitted through the myths of Ishtar/Tammuz and Isis/Osiris, to the gnostic myth of Sophia and her bridegroom, Christ. In the fairy tale, the ancient myth is given a human context, instantly reflecting human experience and human emotions, although the archetypal structure is present throughout. The images of the radiant fairy godmother, together with the motherless daughter, Cinderella, and the prince who chooses her for his bride, suggest that the story belongs to the mystical wisdom tradition enshrined in the marvelous poetry of the Song of Songs, which was derived from the texts of the sacred marriage rituals between goddess and god celebrated in the temples of Egypt, Babylonia, and Sumeria. In the fairy tale, the Mother Goddess of the pre-Christian and gnostic past has become the fairy godmother, mistress of the art of transformation and of all the "disguises" worn by the eternal life-spirit. Cinderella, in her servitude and despair and her blackened rags, knows nothing of this godmother–"her true mother"–or her power to transform sorrow into joy, darkness into light. Her tears call to mind Sophia's lament in the gnostic *Pistis Sophia*, which in turn echoes the words of the Shulamite in the Song of Songs:

> And I was in that place, mourning and seeking the Light that I had seen on high. And the watchman of the gates of the Aeons sought me, and all those who stay within their Mystery mocked me . . . Now, O Light of Lights, I am afflicted in the darkness of the chaos . . . Deliver me out of the matter of this darkness, so that I shall not be submerged in it . . . My strength looked up from the midst of the chaos and from the midst of the darknesses, and I waited for my spouse that he might come and fight for me.[1]

---

[1]Compare the passage in the Song of Songs: "The Watchmen that went about the city found me, they smote me, they wounded me; the keepers of the walls took away my veil from me. I charge you, O daughters of Jerusalem, if ye find my beloved, that ye tell him, that I am sick of love" (5:7,8).

Cinderella, like Sophia and Persephone in earlier myths, cries out in her distress to her mother in the invisible, "transcendent" world. As in the Greek myth where Hermes descends to Persephone, so in the gnostic one, the Virgin Mother Sophia, in response to her daughter's cry for help, sends her son, Christ, to rescue his sister. Her son is the embodiment of Light and Wisdom, who descends into the darkness of his parents' furthest creation to awaken his sister to remembrance of her true nature and divine origin. In the fairy tale, the godmother responds to the call for help with her gift of the power of transformation, which brings Cinderella to the meeting with the prince, and after the lunar three days' "trial" or "darkness," to the royal marriage.

What echoes there are, in this myth, of the descent of the Sumerian Inanna into the dark underworld of her sister goddess Ereshkigal, her three days' "death" or severance from the light, starry world of her origin, and her "resurrection" after her rescue by Enki, the god of wisdom. In Sophia's exile, there is also the resonance of Eve's expulsion from the garden of Eden, and suddenly this biblical myth becomes transparent to the image of the soul's "fall" into unconsciousness or separation as, responding to the urging of the serpent – the primordial image of wisdom and immortality – she chooses to leave the paradise of the garden and embark on her evolutionary journey.

In the gnostic myth of Sophia, the soul is personified for the first time as the daughter of the Mother Goddess and Father God. In one of several versions of the myth, Sophia is the Virgin Mother Goddess, named as the power of wisdom through which life brings itself into being; the womb which generates as her child, all worlds and levels of being. Like the Shekhinah of the Kabbalah, she personifies and radiates light as the informing energy of these worlds. The Mother Sophia gives birth to a daughter, the image of herself, who descends into these worlds, but loses contact with her heavenly origin, and in her distress and sorrow brings the earth into being, at the same time becoming lost or entangled in the realm of darkness that lies beneath the realm of light. A curtain or veil comes between the worlds of light and darkness, making it impossible for her to return to her Mother and Father. She is condemned to wander in this dark labyrinth, "laboring her passion into matter, her yearning into soul" (Jonas 1958, p. xiii). The imagery of this late creation myth is very similar to that of the Shekhinah and the emanations of the Sefiroth, and there is a close parallel between the exiled Sophia and the exiled Shekhinah, who are both cut off from the divine world of their origin. There may even be a Kabbalistic source for certain elements of the story, for the "widower" in Kabbalah was Yahweh himself, deprived of the radiance of his wife, the Shekhinah, and married in her absence to Lilith (Patai 1967, p. 239). The myth of Sophia was used by the gnostics as a metaphor to explain how the soul, the divine "spark" of the cosmic soul, her Mother, is "lost" in her creation – the manifest world – retaining no memory of her pleromatic "home." There is hardly to be found a more graphic image of the human experience of the separation of consciousness from the source, or ground of its being:

> Sometimes she mourned and grieved,
> For she was left alone in darkness and the void;
> Sometimes she reached a thought of the light which had left her,
> And she was cheered and laughed;
> Sometimes she feared;
> At other times she was perplexed and astonished.[2]

So much has been lost with the passage of the centuries, and only now, in this century, can it be recovered and the fragments pieced together. The familiar Cinderella of the fairy tale may seem far removed from this gnostic myth of Sophia weeping in her exile from her Mother and Father in the heavenly dimension. The figure of Cinderella does not immediately suggest the black Shulamite of the Song of Songs, nor does her godmother evoke the Mother Sophia of the starry heavens or the shining radiance of the Shekhinah. Yet a knowledge of mythology and history suggests that a relationship between them cannot be fortuitous. In this tale, as in "Sleeping Beauty" and "Snow White," the gnos-

---

[2]Robert M. Grant, *Gnosticism: An Anthology* (London: Collins, 1961), p. 171. Compare the words of the Naasene hymn:

> Therefore clothed in a watery form, she grieves,
> toy and slave of death,
> Sometimes, invested with royalty, she sees light:
> Sometimes, fallen into evil, she weeps.
> Sometimes she weeps, and sometimes she rejoices;
> Sometimes she weeps, and sometimes she is judged;
> Sometimes she is judged and sometimes she dies.
> Sometimes she finds no exit, because her wandering ways
> Have led to a labyrinth of evils.

From Grant, p. 115.

tic myth and its antecedent Sumerian and Egyptian ones shine through the images and connect the soul receptive to their numinosity with these mythic roots.

The imagery of light is common to the iconography of the goddess in Sumerian, Egyptian, and gnostic myths and to Cinderella as well. Bayley discovered that, etymologically, the syllable *Cin* connects Cinderella with Sin, the Babylonian moon god, father of the goddess Ishtar, whose symbol was the crescent moon. The word Sinai is derived from the same root. *El* in Babylonia was the "light" element in the sun god Bel (Marduk) and in El, the Canaanite father god whose name survives in the Hebrew *Elohim*. *Ella*, as Bayley pointed out, also comes from the Greek *ele* which means shiner or giver of light. *Ele* is the root of Eleusis, as also of *Eleleus*, one of the surnames of Apollo, the god of light, and is also present in *Helios*, the sun, and in *Selene*, the moon (Bayley 1912, p. 192). The word Cinderella as a whole suggests both fire and light, cinders being an earthly analogy of the stars, the fiery sparks glowing in the blackness of the night sky. Jung's passages on the *scintillae* come to mind here, as does the *lumen naturae* of the alchemists, and the starry ground of the soul (the meaning of the word *Compostella*) which was the goal of the pilgrim of the inner world in the Middle Ages (Jung 1954, pars. 388–396).

Fire, light, and the dazzling luminosity of the starry dimension are all images that were associated through the ages with the radiance of wisdom which, as a fusion of love and insight or knowledge, represents the union of Queen and King, the highest feminine and masculine qualities of the soul. In the fairy tale these are personified by Cinderella and the prince. Cinderella's particular quality of sustained devotion to whatever she was asked to do is stressed in every version of the story. The prince's capacity for insight is shown in his recognition of Cinderella and in the tenacity and single-mindedness of his quest for his "true" love.

Paradoxically, wisdom as light may wear the cloak or disguise of blackness, the blackness of the night sky through which the moon shines. Isis wore a black robe and it is wisdom, "black but beautiful," whom the bridegroom in the Song of Songs seeks out as his bride in this ancient recital of the sacred marriage rite. So also did Solomon himself, for to him wisdom was the "brightness of the everlasting light, the unspotted mirror of the power of God, and the image of his goodness" (Wisd. of Sol. 7:26). Wisdom could do all things, "For she is more beautiful than the sun, and above all the order of stars: being compared with the light, she is found before it" (Wisd. of Sol. 7:29). Like the wise men or alchemists who followed the wisdom tradition that originated in Sumeria and was transmitted through Babylonian to Hebrew culture, Solomon loved her and sought her out from his youth: "I desired to make her my spouse, and I was a lover of her beauty" (Wisd. of Sol. 8:2).

Like Solomon, the prince in the story of Cinderella, once having seen her, is consumed with love for her and will have no other as his bride, and she is equally drawn by her love for him. The brother and sister imagery of the Song of Songs as well as the gnostic myth of Sophia rescued by her brother, Christ, is carried through to some versions of the story which are known as "The Brother and Sister." The imagery of light associated with the bridegroom so dramatically portrayed in the gnostic myth is discovered in the Babylonian one where Ishtar is rescued by Uddushu-Namir, whose name means "his light shines" (Jastrow 1898, p. 142). It appears also in the classical myth of Eros and Psyche, for there Eros has "hairs of gold that yielded out a sweet savour, his neck more white than milk, his hair hanging comely behind and before, the brightness whereof did darken the light of the lamp" (Adlington 1566).

As far back as there is knowledge of myth there is the story of the mother/son, sister/brother, wife/husband pair, whose sacred marriage sustains and renews heaven and earth. Separated, they must seek each other. Together they form the image of the whole: dark and light, earth and sky, moon and sun, mother and father, sister and brother, bride and bridegroom—all these form the tapestry of human experience which is the foundation of myth, fairy tale, and religion. One without the other was once inconceivable. The Song of Songs, like the marriage incantations spoken by "goddess" and "god" in the temples of Sumeria and Egypt, celebrated the ecstatic union of the sky goddess with her bridegroom, who was at once her son, her brother, and her lover, and who incarnated the life of nature, her *visible* creation. In Sumeria, the goddess "descended" to her temple, and the ritual of her union with the king ratified his rule by divine sanction. The union of the king, who personified the son-consort, with the high priestess or queen, who personified the goddess, guaranteed the continued fertility of the earth during the coming year. The perennial story of their separation during the "dark" phase of the year and reunion at the time of the return of the earth's fertility is told in the myths of Ishtar and Tammuz in Babylonia, Isis and Osiris in Egypt, as well as in the later ones of Cybele and Attis, Aphrodite and Adonis, and Psyche and Eros. Over some two thousand years, the imagery of the sacred marriage was gradually transformed and interiorized. From being a fertility rite associated with the sacred marriage, as well as the ritual sacrifice of the king or his substitute, whose death gave life to the people, it became, in the Mysteries of Egypt, Greece, and Rome, the celebration of the union of the soul with the divine ground of being. The ground was personified variously by a feminine or masculine deity, depending upon the culture in which the imagery took root.[3] The darkness of the time of separation was associated with the darkness of the soul's sorrow during the time of "exile," and the time of reunion with the idea of return to the source. The sacred marriage and a ritual sacrifice were both central to the Mysteries. In Cinderella they manifest as the royal marriage at the end of the story, and as the bloody amputation of the ugly sisters' toes or heels.

In many versions, apples and honey connect Cinderella with the Song of Songs and with the temple rituals of the sacred marriage. Inanna "knelt by the sacred apple tree" in the marriage ritual of Sumeria (Wolkstein and Kramer 1984, p. 40). In Greece, the golden apples of the Hesperides were Hera's gift, bestowing eternal life. In the Song of Songs, there is the passage: "As the apple trees among the trees of the wood, so is my beloved among the sons" (Song of Songs 2:3). In one version of Cinderella, an apple tree takes the place of the fairy godmother and shakes down from its branches the beautiful dresses that Cinderella wears to the ball. Cinderella, talking to the tree in another version, says:

> Little gold apple tree
> With my vase of gold have I watered thee
> With my spade of gold have I digged thy mould
> Give me your lovely clothes I pray
> And take my ugly rags away.

---

[3]With the Aryan invasions from about 2000 B.C. onwards, the goddess gradually lost her ancient association with the heavens, which originated in the lunar mythology of the Paleolithic and Neolithic eras.

Honey has been associated as far back as Sumeria with the sacred marriage ritual and in Crete with the gift of insight or prophecy and the revelation of the invisible dimension behind the forms of life.[4] It is perhaps the most archaic symbol of wisdom and truth, belonging specifically to the rituals associated with the mysteries of creation and regeneration.

The fairy godmother can be recognized as the Mother Goddess of the pre-Aryan, pre-Christian past. In relation to gnostic myth, she personifies wisdom herself who, as the Mother Sophia, comes to the rescue of her daughter, as Demeter comes to the rescue of Persephone. Cinderella, like the daughter Sophia, is the "image" of her beautiful mother. As the Mother Sophia sends Christ, her son, to help his sister, so the fairy godmother arranges everything so that the prince will fall in love with her daughter, the human soul, and rescue her from a life of drudgery and misery. She is variously described as a queen with a star on her brow, which connects her with Ishtar and Astarte; a cow with golden horns, which recalls Inanna-Ishtar and Isis-Hathor; a wise old woman; a mermaid or a sea serpent who lives in the abyss, which evokes the Babylonian Tiamat and the Sumerian primordial serpent goddess Nammu. In Brazil, she was called "Donna Labismina." Cinderella herself is often called Mara, Maria, or Mariucella, all derived from the root *mare*, which means sea; and the sea, whose distilled essence is the salt of wisdom, is one of the perennial images of the soul.

Transformation is the theme of the story and the alchemist presiding over the great work is wisdom herself who, with a wave of her wand, transforms mice into snow-white horses, lizards into footmen, a pumpkin into the golden (or crystal) coach, a rat into the coachman, and, of course, Cinderella herself into a vision of beauty arrayed in dresses that reflect the radiance of stars, moon, and sun. Cinderella has to do the work of going in search of the animals and vegetable named by her godmother, which suggests that the soul has to respond to wisdom's guidance by identifying the elements to be transformed; once identified and "brought" before the greater insight and power of transformation personified by the godmother, the work of transformation is accom-

---

[4]The priestesses of Apollo and of Artemis, Demeter, and Aphrodite were known as *melissae*—bees—and the chief oracular priestess at Delphi, the *Pythia*, was called "The Delphic Bee."

plished in a flash, although the "twinkling of an eye" of the fairy tale may extend over a lifetime in this dimension. Mice, the animals that scurry about the house in the darkness of the night suggest unconscious thoughts; lizards, unconscious instincts. Mice, as the most fertile of animals, were sacred to the Great Goddess, as well as to the solar gods Horus and Apollo, and were associated with the healing of disease. The lizards—serpents who slough their skins—share this lunar imagery of regeneration with the milk-white color of the horses, but they also suggest the fiery image of the salamander, one of the alchemical symbols of transformation most prominent in fifteenth- and sixteenth-century treatises. The pumpkin's golden color suggests harvest and, in particular, the glow of the harvest moon. The conjunction of the images of gold and harvest reflect, perhaps, the last stage of the alchemical task of transformation, leading to the royal marriage and the union of the soul with spirit. The chariot, fiery, crystal, or golden, is a very ancient symbol which, in Kabbalistic legend, was an image of the Shekhinah as the vehicle of Yahweh, and earlier still, described by Elisha in his vision of Elijah taken up into heaven in a fiery chariot. It was also an image "seen" by the mystic in the course of his spiritual journey. The earliest image of the "heavenly chariot" appears in Bronze Age Crete (the Haghia Triada sarcophogus), where the goddess drives a chariot drawn by griffons, conveying the soul of the deceased to the other world.

The arduousness of the work of transformation is stressed in some versions of Cinderella more than others; for example, in the one where her stepmother throws a heap of seeds onto the ground for the girl to sort into piles. This is identical to the scene in the story of Eros and Psyche, where Psyche is given the same task by her mother-in-law, the goddess Venus, who in this context sets the harsh task which the soul has to accomplish on her journey back to the realm of the gods and her reunion with her husband, Eros. In the classical myth, as in the gnostic one, the bridegroom is the son of the goddess. Doves and birds, whose association with the goddess goes back to the Neolithic era, help Cinderella to sort the seeds and also, in some versions of the story, point out to the prince that a false bride wears the slipper destined for Cinderella, by drawing his attention to the blood flowing from the injured feet of the ugly sisters.

Cinderella's dresses, her "robe of glory," are described as "blue like the sky," "woven of the stars of heaven," of moonbeams, sunbeams, or "made of all the flowers of the world." Sometimes the metaphor of the sea appears and her dress is "sea-colored" or "like the waves of the sea," or "as the sea with fishes swimming in it" and as the "color of sea covered with golden fishes." Sometimes, like Isis, she is robed in jet black; sometimes her dresses shine like the sun or gold, covered in diamonds and pearls, "of splendour passing description," and giving forth the tinkling sound of bells. In one story, Cinderella's dress "rings like a bell as she comes downstairs," which recalls the sistrum of the goddess Isis and also the bells that rang out at the approach of the Shekhinah.[5] But it also reminds one of the description of the robe worn by the initiate in the gnostic poem, "The Hymn of the Robe of Glory": "I heard the sound of its music which it whispered as it descended" (Mead 1906). Cinderella "lets down her hair and shakes out showers of pearls: she is clothed from head to foot with necklaces of brilliants and precious stones, and gems fall from her lips when she speaks." At times she wears "a diamond dress," or a gold dress trimmed with diamonds, or a robe of silk, thread thick with diamonds and pearls" (Bayley 1912, Chaps. 8 and 9). In other versions, Cinderella's dresses are hidden beneath the furry disguise of an animal. In the variation known as Catskin, the king tears off the furry clock made of a thousand animal skins to reveal the shimmering dress hidden beneath it. These marvelous dresses which, in the best-known version are given to Cinderella by her godmother, seem, as Bayley suggests, to symbolize the awakening and growth of wisdom which clothes the soul in ever-greater radiance.

"How beautiful are thy feet with shoes, O prince's daughter!" says the bridegroom in the Song of Songs (Song of Songs 7:1). Cinderella's shoes or slippers are described as made of crystal, or gold or blue glass, or embroidered with pearls. Sometimes they are different on each of the three nights, ending up as gold. Without her glass slipper, Cinderella would not have been recognized, and it could only fit her whose standpoint had been so transformed that it had become translucent to the light of wisdom.

Cinderella is instructed by her godmother to leave the palace before midnight or risk being transformed back into her former state. What could be the meaning of this? Could it be that mid-

[5]See Patai, *The Hebrew Goddess*, Chapter IV, for the Exile of the Shekhinah, and also the Talmudic saying, p. 145: "The Shekhinah rang before him like a bell."

night marks the interface between the dimensions of eternity and time? To fail to hold the balance between them is to risk being fixed in one, unable to relate to or remember the other dimension of experience. To stay at the ball beyond midnight is to forget human values and human relationships, losing touch with physical reality and everyday life. Not to ask to go to the ball is to remain in bondage to material existence, without awareness of the "other" place. The balance between time and eternity must be kept if the sacred marriage is to take place. The hardest task of all is to live in this dimension in the knowledge that it is also "the other," yet cannot be fully experienced as such until consciousness is so transformed that it "sees through" the veil of appearances.

Cinderella's ugly sisters and stepmother may have an ancient history. The contrast between Cinderella and her two sisters may have a Hebrew origin, for Cinderella may be identified with the "true" bride of Yahweh, and the ugly sisters with Israel and Judah, the two Hebrew states which were "unfaithful" to him, returning to the old Canaanite religious rites, and whose fearful fate, falling in bondage to Assyria, is so graphically predicted and described by the prophets in the Old Testament. But the ugly sisters also appear in Apuleius's story of Eros and Psyche, where they play the role of the "false values" which intrude upon her relationship with her divine husband. In the fairy tale, their finery cannot conceal their ugliness, and their feet do not fit the slipper whatever mutilation they inflict on them.

The contrast between the two "mothers" in Cinderella may reflect a gnostic viewpoint. The two mothers may describe the gnostic and orthodox Christian churches. The gnostics, both in the early centuries when the Christian doctrine was being formulated, and in the later Middle Ages, contrasted their "true" teaching with the "false" teaching of the church which did not rescue the soul but prolonged her suffering and exile, keeping her in ignorance of her divine nature and the way to recover her knowledge of herself. In the early centuries of Christianity, the church was named by the Christian Fathers as the Virgin Mother of the faithful and the Bride of Christ. The church therefore assumed the imagery of the former Goddess, as well as the mantle of wisdom that had once belonged to the Holy Spirit, Sophia, the feminine aspect of the divine who was with Yahweh "from the beginning."

> As Virgin and Mother the Church . . . is represented as undefiled by false doctrine and ever loving and watchful of those who come within her affectionate embrace, sanctifying them as children of God, training them on earth and so preparing them to attain to citizenship in heaven. (James 1959, p. 197)

During the centuries of persecution, both in the early centuries of Christianity and later in the Middle Ages, although claiming to be the "Mother of the Faithful," the church became the very antithesis of the true mother, wisdom, whose image was associated with the gnostic church. No one who has studied the history of religious persecution can fail to be aware of the Church as the "Terrible Mother" and the horror of the centuries when one's neighbor could not be trusted for fear of betrayal to the Inquisition.

In the tale of Snow White, there is the same contrast between the "true" mother who dies, and the "false" mother, the wicked queen who transforms herself into an old hag and brings Snow White the poisoned or death-bringing "gifts," including the poisoned apple that sticks in her throat and causes her to fall into a deathlike trance. The prince who awakens her with a kiss and restores her to life evokes the image of the gnostic Christ who is sent to rescue his sister from her "sleep" in the world.

So many elements from earlier cultures are present in this story that it is impossible to say when and where it may have originated. One thing is certain: its importance to the soul is shown by the universality and duration of its appeal. Cinderella tells the story of a single theme that runs from the mythology of Sumeria and Egypt to the mysteries of the pagan world and the Wisdom literature of Judaism. It can be followed through gnosticism and mystical Christianity to alchemy, the grail legends, and the most cherished fairy tales. It was nurtured by the mystics of the Jewish, Christian, and Muslim religions. It is the story of the soul's "descent" into the manifest world, her loss of memory of her divine origin, her quest for understanding of herself and her relationship to the divine "source" or "world" from which she had emanated and to which, in full knowledge of who she is, she may return. Who is the fairy godmother but Sophia herself, Divine Wisdom, the Holy Spirit—mother, source, and womb—the light and intelligence that is the very ground of the soul? Who else should preside as godmother over her daughter's quest for insight, illumination, and union? Responding to Cinderella's call for help, she initiates the work of transformation, making possible her meeting with the prince, and bringing her, after the lunar three days' "trial" or "darkness," to the royal marriage. The tale of Cinderella tells the story of the soul's transfiguration as she is changed from soot-blackened drudge into radiant bride.

The image of the soul's journey weaves like a golden thread through mythology and literature that spans five thousand years. It first appears in Sumeria, when Inanna, Queen of Heaven and Earth, surrenders her glorious apparel at each of the seven gates on her way to the underworld kingdom of her sister, Ereshkigal, reassuming them after her three-day crucifixion in darkness as she re-ascends to the light. The soul, as Eve, is banished from the Garden of Eden and goes into exile, as does the "widowed" Shekhinah and the gnostic daughter Sophia. The Cinderella of the fairy tale personifies all these earlier mythic figures who in turn image the human soul and the predicament of the darkened "light" which has no knowledge of itself. As in the stories of the Sleeping Beauty and Snow White, the soul awakens to the kiss of the prince who, as the solar bridegroom, consort of the moon goddess, personifies the divine life principle and, in these stories, the highest potential of human consciousness. The archaic imagery of the sacred marriage is concealed in the relationship of the Virgin and Christ, who crowns his mother as his bride, and is developed in alchemy, infusing the poetry and legends of the Middle Ages with the urgent beauty of the soul's quest for wisdom – "Notre Dame" – in whose honor the magnificent cathedrals of Europe arose. The theme pervades the grail legends, the *Romaunt de la Rose*, and Dante's great allegory of the soul's awakening and return to her source. The artists of the Renaissance, steeped in the hermetic knowledge of Marsilio Ficino, proclaim Mary as the awakened soul seated in the midst of the garden, fragrant with the lilies and the roses which are wisdom's timeless symbols. Impregnated by the Divine Spirit, she has brought forth her "son." So also the alchemist labored to transform himself as lover of wisdom, into her son, the *filius philosophorum*, or *filius Sophiae* – as he would have named her, if he had dared.

What is the cultural relevance of the story of Cinderella in the new age that is dawning? The image of the sacred marriage between nature and spirit, goddess and god, has been notably absent in the Judeo-Christian tradition and this has inflicted a deep wound on the psyche which has yet to be healed. The fairy tale restores the image of union between the two primary archetypes and has, so to speak, "carried" it for our culture until such time as the need for it could become conscious. The slow emergence in human consciousness of the plight of the feminine archetype embraces the image of the soul's suffering and ignorance of herself, and of an earth and nature that, split off from spirit, are also suffering and in need of rescue. Cinderella personifies these three aspects of the feminine value so long relegated to the role of servant. The "resurrection" of this archetype has been prepared for many centuries by those who often sacrificed their lives to the transmission of the wisdom tradition – "black but beautiful" – so that it would not vanish into oblivion. It may even have been one of them – whether Jew, Christian, or Muslim – who first imagined this fairy tale, drawing on the repository of myth inherited by the mystical tradition of all three cultures from their Sumerian, Egyptian, and gnostic past. This tradition taught the immanence of the divine in nature and human nature. It emphasized the need to discover the presence of the radiant essence hidden within the myriad forms of life and the "darkness" of unreflecting human consciousness. They would each have recognized – as Harold Bayley did – that Cinderella, "the bright and shining one, who sits among the cinders and keeps the fire alight," is the "personification of the Holy Spirit dwelling unhonoured amid the smouldering ashes of the Soul's latent, never totally extinct, Divinity" (Bayley 1912, pp. 194–195).

REFERENCES

Adlington, W. 1566. *The Golden Ass*. London: Loeb Classical Library, 1915.

Bayley, H. 1912. *The Lost Language of Symbolism*. London: Williams and Norgate.

Cox, M. R. 1893. *Cinderella*. London: The Folklore Society.

Grant, R. M. 1961. *Gnosticism: An Anthology*. London: Collins.

James, E. O. 1959. *The Cult of the Mother Goddess*. London: Thames and Hudson.

Jastrow, M. 1898. *The Religion of Babylonia and Assyria*. New York: Atheneum Press.

Jonas, H. 1958. *The Gnostic Religion*. Boston: Beacon Press.

Jung, C. G. 1954. On the nature of the psyche. *CW* 8:159–235. Princeton, N.J.: Princeton University Press, 1960.

Mead, G. R. S., trans. 1906. *Fragments of a Faith Forgotten*. London: John M. Watkins.

Patai, R. 1967. *The Hebrew Goddess*. New York: Ktav Publishing House, Inc.

Wolkstein, D., and Kramer, S. N. 1984. *Inanna*. London: Rider and Co., Ltd.

"Cupid and Psyche" Birth of a New Consciousness

Lena B. Ross

THE NATURE OF TALES

Every myth and fairy tale tells us about psychic processes. Some symbolically depict ways that the psyche develops and survives. A few, however, describe particularly "healthy" development. Among the latter is the fairy tale "Cupid and Psyche," incorporated by Lucius Apuleius in his book *Metamorphoses* or *The Golden Ass*.[1] This fairy tale delineates the struggle to separate from the collective while maintaining a relationship to the divine.[2] The tale examines also the prospective function of the archetypes and the ways in which they themselves develop.

---

[1]Apuleius never uses either "Amor" or "Eros," but always "Cupid"; I shall do the same, respecting the choice of the author as meaningful. John Winkler lodges a narratological protest at the title "Cupid and Psyche," as no title is given in the Latin text. However, the two names eventually used are Cupidus and Psyche, so at least there is some reason to refer to the tale this way. I lodge my own protest, however, at the continuous use among commentators of either "Amor" or "Eros." These names apparently satisfy the twentieth-century need to bow to prejudices at the connotations now of "Cupid." But even a cursory reading of tales about this god will show him to have been feared by all the other gods. This is no mischievous cherub!

[2]I am using "fairy tale" here in the sense of the German word *Märchen*, which H. J. Rose uses as distinct from "myth" or "saga." In the excellent introduction to his *Handbook of Greek Mythology*, he says that this word fits better than

One issue illuminated by "Cupid and Psyche" is that of certain patients who do not improve in analysis. Balint designates them as fixated at a preverbal level where no objects exist. Transference cannot be formed, therefore analysis is prevented. There are "no objects in the area of creation [but] we know that the subject is not entirely alone there. The trouble is that our language has no words to describe, or even to indicate, the 'somethings' that are there" (Balint 1968, p. 25).

There is and always has been such a language, however, the language of symbols. Understanding symbolic language enables us to comprehend underlying patterns and possibilities. Further, Balint's concept of a level where no objects exist, yet "the subject is not entirely alone," can be understood as a space where an individual identity has not differentiated out of the totality of the Self. This dynamic is expressed quite clearly through "Cupid and Psyche," which Jack Lindsay describes as "at root a folktale [which] belongs to the tale type of the Beast-Lover" (Apuleius 1932, p. 20).

Cupid and Psyche

Psyche's great beauty caused her to be worshipped as a goddess. Venus became angry and directed her son Cupid to cause Psyche to fall in love with the most degraded of men.

Psyche was unhappy. Although men worshipped her, none loved her. Her father consulted the oracle of Apollo which said that Psyche would wed a terrifying being. Sadly, Psyche's parents led her to await the monster. Instead, she is wafted to a palace where invisible hands wait on her and an invisible husband makes love to her at night. Although forbidden to see him, she is happy. Her sisters, meanwhile, look for her, loudly lamenting. Psyche, hearing them becomes restless and asks to see her sisters. Her husband

---

"the nearest English equivalent, 'fairytale,' because it does not always deal with fairies." He notes further that in the classification of legends (into myth, saga, and *Märchen*), "any given story might very well combine two of these, or even all three." Rose firmly places "Cupid and Psyche" into this group. More than anything else, though, it is the style in which this tale is written that places it into the category of *Märchen*, as Rose defines this: the quality of amusement, a tale told for the entertainment of the audience, not simply its edification (Rose 1959, pp. 13–14).

says no, but Psyche prevails. Meanwhile, her husband informs her that she is pregnant.

Filled with envy, her two sisters plot to destroy her happiness. They convince her that her husband is a deadly serpent. Psyche takes an oil lamp to see him at night while he is asleep. She sees the beautiful god of love, Cupid, and experiences terror, then fascination. Handling his arrows, she accidently pricks her finger. This causes her to burn with desire for Cupid; but a drop of oil falls from the lamp and burns him. Waking in agony, he flies away. Psyche attempts suicide but the river into which she throws herself refuses to accept her life.

Psyche encounters Pan embracing Echo. He advises her to show adoration to Cupid to win him back. Without answering, Psyche wanders off, going first to her sisters and, leading them to believe that Cupid wants them instead of her, tricks each into throwing herself over a cliff in the belief that she will be caught by the West Wind; each dies.

Psyche, hiding from Venus, searches for Cupid. Venus, looking for Psyche, enlists the aid of Mercury, who disseminates notice of Venus's reward. Psyche gives herself up and is tortured.

Venus next assigns impossible tasks to Psyche: sorting a large pile of seeds, collecting wool from the rams of the sun, and filling a flask from dangerous waters. Each time, Psyche is magically helped.

Venus gives her a fourth task: to ask Proserpina to fill the box of beauty. A tower assists Psyche, instructing her in avoiding traps set by Venus and warning her not to open the box of beauty. Psyche disobeys, opens the box, and collapses into unconsciousness; she is then rescued by Cupid. They both ascend to heaven, where Psyche, immortalized, gives birth to a daughter named Voluptas.

Psychological interpretations of this tale have varied: Neumann (1956) interprets it as pertaining to feminine psychological development, while von Franz (1980) and Ulanov (1971) choose to interpret it as relating to masculine anima development. Hillman (1972) and Durand (1981) view it as representing a large archetypal schema, an approach with which I concur as the tale subsumes the categories of contrasexual components of psychological development.

By considering the explicit or denotative meaning of the Latin text rather than the associative or connotative meaning, I hope to shed light on the archetypal organization of the text as well as on areas such as the oracle of Apollo, the Pan/Echo section, Voluptas, and the function of desire in individuation.[3]

The development of Cupid provides a striking feature of the tale. In the Roman pantheon, Cupid, son of Venus, creates love between others.[4] Nowhere do the various tales about Cupid indicate that he feels love *himself* until he meets Psyche. One significant aspect of this tale, then, is the fact that the archetypal energy represented by Cupid—desire—is a force that both provokes change (in Psyche) and changes in itself. Cupid develops from a figure detached from the drama of felt love into a committee actor. In this story, an archetypal pattern unfolds in symbolic language which creates transformation by way of the energy of desire.

THE NATURE AND FUNCTION OF DESIRE

In the tale, Psyche is seen as Venus. The multitudes flock to gaze on her as though she were one of the wonders of the world. This identification with Venus is her lot and only when she is sacrificed to the unknown monster does she begin to realize it.

Clinically, this reflects a growth and development of the infant psyche which is an unfolding not of its potential, but rather of the wishes of family and society. It is easy to misread this form of psyche as a false self-organization of a far too collective persona.

Psyche's story represents the emergence of identity cohering out of genetic and psychic givens, her prima materia. There is not a hidden spark or true core that must be integrated in order to overcome falseness; it can be disastrous to view patients through the lens of the false self, when Psyche's tale constitutes the appropriate metaphor. Psyche's story shows us the birth of a new self,

---

[3]Three good translations of the Latin are by Adlington (1566), Butler (1910), and Lindsay (1932). My favorite is Lindsay's. Occasionally, I will use my own translation when I feel extant translations are not adequately clear.

[4]There is a structural problem in seeing this tale as pertaining primarily to the man's relationship to his anima. It is Cupid who is the god, Psyche the mortal. As such, it is Cupid whose energies would be archetypal, not Psyche, so that it is difficult to see her as representing the archetype of the anima, while viewing Cupid as representing a man.

forged out of her pain and her growing capacity to disobey.

When viewed psychologically as it relates to the character Psyche, this tale pertains to those patients who are fused with the Self and have a functional pseudo-ego. Lloyd, a rock musician without formal training, was a "natural" through whom music came directly from the Self with little ego to mediate it. His identity depended on fusing with a four-member band, without which he felt empty and anxious; he would sleep all day when the band was not active. This marginal existence never allowed him a workable relationship with an "other." I often envisioned him dangling from a bank of clouds, legs kicking for support that was not there.

Other patients, who have attributes such as beauty or wealth, can develop an acceptable persona and functional ego. So much is projected into these people by others that they can succeed for a time until, crushed by the weight of collective projections running counter to a sense of inner emptiness, they fail to establish relationships or hold a good job.

One patient, Rosa, reported that in an interview she would often do remarkably well, getting hired for jobs for which she had no training. Rosa told of losing such jobs when her employers found that she could not do them, but she was hopelessly tied into the projections aroused by her queenly beauty and frightened of confronting her suspicion that inside there was nothing at all. She had no opportunity to develop anything but an ego made up of collectively approved attributes.

Psyche's beauty provokes anger in Venus; symbolically, this highlights the ambivalence of the Self, which both wants incarnation and at the same time does not easily allow it. The biological analogue is the pain of birth: presumably, nature could have devised painless reproduction, but birth begins in pain for both mother and infant. To forge an ego out of the overwhelming, chaotic vastness of the Self requires consciously chosen suffering. Psyche suffers: in the beginning of the tale, we are told that Psyche

> had no joy of her loveliness. All men gazed on her, yet never a king nor prince nor even a lover from the common folk came forward desirous to claim her hand in marriage. Men marveled at her divine loveliness, but as men marvel at a statue fairly wrought. (Neumann 1956, p. 6)

Long after her sisters were wed, "Psyche sat at home an unwedded maid and, sick of body and broken in spirit, bewailed her loneliness and solitude" (ibid.). This suffering, however, is not meaningful, because the desire remains impersonal. It could be ended, presumably, by a suitor—any suitor.

Meanwhile Venus, enraged at the incarnation of her beauty in a mortal, summons her son and instructs him to make Psyche fall in love with the most *extreme of men* (*extremus homo*), someone low and degraded. Her ambivalence here is striking: she does not command him to kill Psyche, nor does she do so herself. And we must wonder about the meaning of why this goddess sends her beloved son to see the most beautiful woman in the world without a thought about what effect that beauty might have on him.

The oracle of Apollo, however, decrees a different fate: Psyche will wed a *terrible being*. As Winkler indicates, our attention seems deliberately drawn to this disparity when Psyche says, "Now I realize, now I see that I have been doomed to die for being called Venus" (1985, p. 91). Psyche believes the identification with Venus to be the sole cause of her impending doom. As yet able to see only part of the truth, Psyche remains a victim.

A crucial moment in analysis occurs when a patient can finally experience the real pain of his or her childhood. Unlike Psyche at this point in the tale, the patient then must take the further step of leaving the security, however painful it might have been, that the early situation provided. The oracle of Apollo promotes Psyche's salvation, since she will ultimately manifest a separate identity through consciously chosen suffering.

The oracle decrees a bridegroom for Psyche so powerful that the gods tremble before him. A psychological reading provides more clarity here than a narratological one: it is Cupid who is

> Fierce and wild and of the dragon breed/He swoops all-conquering, born on airy wing,/With fire and sword he makes his harvesting;/ Trembles before him Jove, whom gods do dread,/And quakes the darksome river of the dead. (Neumann 1956, p. 7)

While Venus rules over desire and love, only Cupid *creates* desire between others. Therefore Cupid can make fools of the gods. As Venus says to Cupid, "You rule the Gods, and Jove himself" (Ovid, V, 368–369). Apollo's decree tacitly acknowledges

Cupid's power.[5] As the tale goes on, the necessity for Psyche to fulfill a purpose more far-reaching than that of Venus becomes apparent. *Apollo's oracle is sanctioning nothing less than the birth of consciousness out of the chaos of the unconscious through the medium of desire, before which even the gods tremble.*

THE FUNCTION OF DISOBEDIENCE IN INDIVIDUATION

Psyche can only differentiate out of her identification with Venus via her link with another part of the archetypal realm, Cupid, for whom she feels desire. Disobedience, the mode of Psyche's differentiation, is as heroic as Hercules. But where Hercules' labors represent a more standard type of heroism, Psyche's is different, as when she rejects projections of the godhead.

Hercules and Psyche are two of only a very few mortals to be granted translation to heaven by Jove. They achieved their immortality via successful trials. Many stories tell of the gods' desire to grant eternal youth and/or immortality to their favorites; the results are usually negative, as in the story of Tithonus, for whom Aurora's intercession failed, as he was granted immortality but not eternal youth (Ovid, IX, 421).[6] As Jove stresses, "Does anyone suppose that he can so far prevail as to alter Fate's decrees? . . . You, too . . . and me the Fates control" (Ovid, IX, 427 *passim*).

Psyche's story, her impulsive disobedience, represents the driving impulse toward individuation. Neumann cites "the uncon-

---

[5]As well he might—for in Ovid's *Metamorphoses*, finished in A.D.7, Ovid recounts a conversation between Apollo and Cupid, in which Apollo pompously directs Cupid to put aside his bow and arrow, bragging about his own accomplishments and instructing Cupid to be "content with thy torch to light the fires of love, and lay not claim to my honours." Cupid's reply: "Thy dart may pierce all else, Apollo, but mine shall pierce thee; and by as much as all living things are less than deity, by so much less is thy glory than mine." True to his word and his power, Cupid then shoots the arrows which both kindle passion in Apollo and repulsion in Daphne (Ovid, 1, 453).

[6]One exception, Ganymede, is in a different position: because of his beauty, he is brought to Olympus specifically to be cupbearer to the gods. Since he has an assigned purpose that is not out of line with his "job" as a human being—to serve the gods—he does not seem like a genuine example of a mortal made into a god; although he is granted eternal life and youth because of his beauty, he has no assigned powers or sector of which he could be called the ruling principle (Hesiod, 421).

sciousness of [Psyche's] situation," referring to her speaking "negatively of the darkness" and "her desire to know her lover" (1956, p. 76). This unconsciousness is a trap: there is no way to exist in space/time within a perfect womb, the paradise of unconsciousness in which Psyche finds herself.

Caryn, a young mother of thirty-five, lived in an expensive house in the country. She had married young; her husband worked hard, successfully establishing himself in banking. She raised the children while he supported them. As the fourteen years of their marriage passed, she found herself dependent on him in every way. She became accustomed to the luxury of her life; when it turned out that he was an abusive alcoholic, she felt stuck.

The "stuckness" was partly economic, but also psychic: "invisible" hands gave her everything. But in this totally unconscious environment, she developed a malformation in her brain which threatened to take her life at an early age. Caryn's story underlines the crucial nature of disobedience in Psyche's tale: Psyche's inability to "obey," in contrast to Caryn's, her impulses which *seem* self-destructive, have a prospective function for individuation.

Psyche's life in this paradise is altered when her husband takes her virginity in the dark. Symbolically, the ending of virginity and the planting of seeds within represents a change in an inner state. This marriage of the human with the divine signals a fusion with the unconscious. Into this "paradise" enter the evil sisters, who, coming to mourn Psyche's death, instead are wafted to her by the West Wind. Her husband foresees the danger of their contamination, but nevertheless accedes to her wishes.

The sisters are able to convince Psyche that her husband is a serpent waiting to devour her and her unborn child. Psychologically, the threat is real that the human and its products can be eaten by the divine. In the state in which the archetype remains here, no human growth is possible. Cupid even tempts Psyche thus: "You, child as you are, yet bear a child in your womb. If you keep your peace concerning our secret, that child will be divine. If you profane our secret, it will be mortal" (Apuleius 1932, p. 116).

Only Jove, however, has the power to raise a human to immortality. Since there were demigods in both the Roman and Greek pantheons, the child of Cupid and Psyche, a god and a mortal, would normally be one of these. Is Cupid lying? Or luring

Psyche with a promise to keep her unconscious? No wonder she believes her sisters!

In any case, Psyche disobeys – when she seeks to know her lover by sight, she discovers the beautiful god of love. In the lunar mode, the knowledge of love exists: Psyche can feel Cupid at night. But light represents solar consciousness. Since Cupid tries to deny Psyche the light, her disobedience means seizing it for herself against the expressed wishes of the archetype. In the differentiation of ego out of prima materia, the integration of lunar and solar elements becomes essential for consciousness. Thus, her sisters represent crucial elements for individuation, not merely agents provocateur for her destruction.

When Psyche obtained her first glimpse of her husband by the light of the oil lamp, "she was terrified at the sight. She lost all self-control . . . and swooning, pallid and trembling, she sought to hide the knife – deep in her own bosom" (Apuleius 1932, p. 121). But then Psyche feels spellbound and worshipful at the sight of his beauty. These opposites are the two extremes of a spectrum experienced by the human in unmediated contact with the *numinosum*. For Psyche, the prick of Cupid's arrow becomes the mediating and releasing factor; but when Psyche's desire is at its fullest a drop of oil falls from the lamp, awakening Cupid.

In pain and furious at her betrayal, he punishes her by flying away. Her desire, now object-oriented, spurs Psyche on in a way that her unconscious union with him could not. As Jung says, "for always the ardour of love transmutes fear and compulsion into a higher free type of feeling" (cited by Hillman 1972, p. 95). Psyche then attempts suicide, throwing herself into the river, which, unwilling to accept her, returns her to the river bank.

Wandering off, she encounters the god Pan, embracing the nymph Echo. Although short, the event is a subtle and powerful moment in the story. There are some striking differences in translation, as well as a lack of commentary on this section. When it is mentioned, it is usually with high praise for Pan but without understanding of the mythological relationship of Pan and Echo.

This section begins, "*Tunc forte Pan deus rusticus iuxta supervilium amnis sedebat, complexus Echo montanam deam,*" usually translated, "Then Pan, the rustic god, was seated by the riverbank embracing Echo, goddess of the mountains." It is the latter part of this sentence for which there are some puzzling translations, explanations, or omissions. While "*voculas omnimodas edocens recinere*" is most often translated as Pan teaching

Echo to tune her instruments, sing, or echo, the Latin makes no mention of instruments. While *voculas* refers to a small or feeble voice, or a soft note or tone, and one meaning of *recinere* is "to sing again," the emphasis here lies on a more exact meaning of *recinere*, to cause to resound, relating to Echo's need to have an effect on her environment.

Echo has a little voice that cannot cause her environment to respond adequately. The use of *recinere* rather than *resonare* or *vocem redere*, words which also mean echo or re-echo, but do not carry the particular meaning, "to cause to resound," implies that this ability was one that Echo ought to have but cannot manifest.[7] Clinically, this makes far more sense than simply learning to echo, even in the sense of harmony with the environment, particularly as the echo was a curse imposed by Juno for Echo's protection of Jove while he cavorted with the nymphs (Ovid, III, 358). Echo's situation relates to patients who have only a collective identity: the prima materia nevertheless contains the instinctual imprinting for an individual voice.

With regard to the Echo/Narcissus myth and its relevance to the narcissistic personality disorder, Nathan Schwartz-Salant points to the importance of echoing by the analyst in the session: "When the analyst echoes back the patient's controlling comments, he must do so with an implicit understanding of the archetypal . . . background," and "the therapist must be capable of echoing in the divine and not the profane sense" (1982, p. 84). Most importantly, he says "the analyst's mirroring is most effective when it is *embodied*" (ibid., p. 85). These statements find their parallel in the emphasis in this tale on the development of the *patient's* voice, with its ability to have an effect on its surrounding environment, not solely because of environmental givens like beauty.

Psyche's ability to evoke resonance from her environment only as a result of her identification with Venus meant that feelings generated by the *numinosum*, awe and worship, acted to separate her from ordinary human life. Her own "voice" had been feeble. Clinically, amplification of one's inner voice constitutes the counterpart to one's inner vision. It is initially an ego task par

---

[7]This manuscript was read prior to publication by Professor Mark Petrini and Professor Ellen Finkelperl, Dept. of Classics, Columbia University, New York City. They gave generously of their time and attention, offering valuable comments on this paper, particularly on the Latin throughout.

excellence, and the sight of Echo being taught by Pan how to amplify her voice in all kinds of ways might be mistakenly understood psychologically as a positive action of the Self, were it not for the mythological underpinning of the Pan/Echo relationship.

Pan seduced Echo before her sad encounter with Narcissus (Nonnos, II, 118). Another story tells how Pan became angry at Echo's wish to stay virginal; feeling "envious of her music because he could not have her beauty," he punished her by sending "a madness among the shepherds and goatherds, and they in a desparate fury . . . tore her all to pieces and flung about them all over the earth her yet singing limbs" (Longus, III, 24).[8] These and other tales of Pan do not portray him as a god who would foster individuality. It sounds like Pan used Echo as he did many nymphs; he is not exactly an altruistic god! The mythology of Pan does not support the view of him as a helpful instructor, and Apuleius's presentation of Pan may be understood as a subtle irony.

Psyche does not thank Pan for his advice to win Cupid back by adoration and obedience. Instead, "she gave no answer, but made reverence unto him as a god and so departed" (Apuleius 1566, p. 237). The story of Echo and Pan represents a failed attempt at an individuation process, one which would lead Psyche, if she followed Pan's advice, to remain undifferentiated in her adoration of Cupid. Psyche's silence in the face of Pan's advice indicates that her individuality is already manifesting.

Psyche is all mortal (where Echo is not) and thus may be seen as more embodied – and the body is important in this tale, as the emphasis on beauty tells us. Wallace Stevens expresses a similar meaning to that which is implicit in the fairy tale: "Beauty is momentary in the mind/the fitful tracing of a portal/but in the flesh it is immortal./The body dies, the body's beauty lives" (1959, p. 5). If Echo represents an attempt psychologically at "the connection between the ego and the archetypal world" (Schwartz-Salant 1982, p. 84), then that attempt fails. Although Pan advises Psyche that Cupid must be wooed with adoration, Echo's

---

[8]The complete story can be found in Longus's novel, *Daphnis and Chloe*, but passing references to Pan's "affair" with Echo can be found in other classical texts. One intriguing story cited in the Roscher Lexicon, V.I,1214, says that Pan's unrequited love for Echo was given to him as a curse by Aphrodite. I have not been able to trace this story, but find its implications intriguing in terms of this fairy tale.

tragic end indicates that adoration is neither efficacious nor sufficient. Psyche's task is to develop a voice that will speak for her in the world.

The need to manifest a voice appears often in therapy. One woman spent her first three years struggling to manifest a cohesive ego out of prima materia parts that had been preserved separately in multiple personality form. Then a further effort began to give birth to a self that would live out of her being and not out of the perceived expectations of others. Without this last part of the opus, she could still be tortured endlessly by her replication on the inner level of her abandonment by a mother and father who both felt helpless and despairing. What she heard from inner voices representing the parents was, "You have no rights." Her child's silent response, "I musn't speak."

Another patient, who expressed disgust at her feelings of inner emptiness and weakness, began to recognize feelings of abandonment by a passive, drunken father. She remembered striking him hard across the face—and receiving no response even to this! Describing her effect on others, she said, "I'm like a housefly buzzing around—just an irritant, with no real effect."

THE PROSPECTIVE FUNCTION OF THE DARKER ELEMENTS

Psyche wanders next to her sisters' houses where she causes their deaths by using guile for the first time. Psychologically this means that through a great shock, the ego shifts into the integration of the shadow. Clinically, experiential recognition of shadow is quite difficult: the shadow is the archetype that embodies all we do not know or own about ourselves. Although Jung describes the shadow as "the most accessible of archetypes and the easiest to experience" (1948; par. 13), he warns against the propensity of the unconscious to play tricks and prevent a real confrontation: "A patient may see the darkness in himself for a moment but the next moment he tells himself he is not so bad after all" (1959, par. 885).

Psyche's envious sisters can manipulate her because she acts out of a collective dynamic that requires her to naively provoke envy without being adequately wise to meet its consequences. Psyche now can be seen with the power of her shadow at the service of an emerging ego, which will lend her the dimensionality to undertake further trials and tribulations.

Experiencing the confrontation with shadow elements of one's personality feels shattering, but, as Fordham points out, it is vital to undergo "the direct experience of early infantile events felt in a very primitive way to be good or bad" (1965). As Hubback (1972, p. 154) notes, envy comes out of a stage in the infant's life where the possibility of deprivation exists. If the infant's cries are not answered, then splitting off of affective response along with a draining of the capacity for affective liveliness might ensue. Clinically, this is not uncommon: a particular type of patient will manifest a kind of affective paralysis rather than an object-oriented rage.

Psyche's revenge might seem extreme; however, she does suddenly come into a kind of ego power which she had been lacking. Without the depth that shadow elements give her, it is doubtful whether she would be able to meet the much larger rage of Venus.

Psyche continues on her journey, "resolute in quest of Cupid" (Apuleius 1932, p. 125). She seeks shelter at the shrines of Ceres and Juno, but both refuse her succor because of their close ties with Venus. Symbolically, the archetypal can no longer rescue the human, as in times past, when the human could appeal for divine intervention. The attitude of the two goddesses remains neutral, so Psyche continues to try and find a way to hide.

Meanwhile, Venus appeals to Jupiter for Mercury's help in proclaiming on Earth a reward for finding Psyche: seven kisses and one "more sweetly honeyed from the touch of her honeyed tongue" (Apulieus 1566, p. 261). Here is the seduction of the uncontained erotic impulses – as Hillman says, "Eros is always somewhat psychotic and psychopathic; in love we must be mad" (1972, p. 101). The obsession of a patient with a love object often seems like madness – all of the energy that could go to living out an individual inner plan remains bound in the love object. The madness is attached to incest desire, when Psyche marries Cupid and must stay in the dark; when the marriage is a secret from all the world, it is a symbolic representation of the incest drive.

One of the ways that this power can begin to be dislodged is through constellation of the eros in the patient/analyst dyad; this contains the unleashed erotic energies and promotes change. Jung recognized this as an underlying pattern: in his essay, "Symbols of the Mother and Rebirth," he writes,

> the basis of the incestuous desire is not cohabitation, but . . . the strange idea of becoming a child again, . . . of entering into the mother in order to be reborn through her. *But the way to this goal lies through incest*, i.e., the necessity of finding some way into the mother's body. (1952, par. 332, italics mine)

Cupid's retreat to his mother's house and Psyche's voluntary return to Venus constitute such a return to the mother's body. Only through the return can Psyche's suffering bring about the new pattern where an

> effect of the incest taboo and of the attempt at canalization [can] stimulate the creative imagination, which gradually opens up possible avenues for the self-realization of libido. (Ibid.)

When incest desire constellates in an analysis, Venusian energy is at its most dangerous: sometimes analysts make the mistake of concretizing the eros and bringing sex into the analysis. At this point the unleashed powers of Venus have entered the analysis and there is little chance that they can be contained; instead, the process of the patient will cease to be the *raison d'etre* of the analysis and chaos of one kind or another ensues.

But Venus's powers cannot be ignored; they will be present, so it is essential for the analyst to understand what is happening in terms of its archetypal underpinnings and to consciously sacrifice the acting out of desire but *with full recognition of the torture of the love*. The sacrifice is a necessary torture–if, like Psyche's choice here, the suffering of the analyst in the countertransference can be consciously chosen and endured, rather than split off, thus abandoning the patient in his or her moment of distress, or acted out by concretizing sexually, the reward at the end can be the transformation of the patient.

The promise of Venus's reward engenders the madness of desire in humans. Psyche stops it by abandoning her attempt to hide and accepting expected death, an acceptance that mirrors her original acquiescence of her fate at the behest of the oracle. The second "death," unlike the first, is actively sought. Instead of death, she finds suffering: she is whipped, beaten, tortured.

Meanwhile, Cupid is "moaning in his mother's bedroom," from the pain of the oil-lamp burn. This retreat to the mother signals a regression of the archetype that parallels Psyche's moments of despair and suicidal thoughts. Formerly "untouchable," Cupid has been penetrated by desire. The entire order of things appears to be upset: a gossipy seagull tells Venus,

> there is no Joy, no Grace, no Elegance anywhere nothing but the Rude, the Rustic, the Uncouth—no Marriage-bond, no Social Intercourse, no Love of Children; nothing but an utter Lack of Order, and an unpleasant Horror of anything so Low as Nuptials. (Apuleius 1932)

As Cupid undergoes a transformation from the unbridled possessor of an enormous power—the ability to create passion—into a being touched by love for a single object, Psyche, both he and the order of things experience something that we are only accustomed to seeing in terms of one god to another: the total disruption of order and functioning, as, for example, when Demeter mourns the loss of Persephone to Hades, and winter comes to Earth.[9]

When Ceres and Juno chastise Venus for denying Cupid's passion for Psyche while scattering the seeds of desire to all nations (*cupidines populis disseminantem*), the psychological implication is the necessity for boundaries and containers to hold and give form to that desire. Venus's energy permeates life: it is not directed at any one source, but is part of a deeply rooted eros-generating center. Cupid represents that energy narrowed down through deliberately aimed arrows—but still used indiscriminantly.

This tale indicates a means through which that larger, unbounded energy might be contained, in this case through the fixing of the energies in the dyad Cupid/Psyche. To use De Rougement's phrase, "passion means suffering," not only for Psyche, but, obviously, for Cupid, too (1983, p. 15). This archetypal energy suffers and changes in its narrowing down to incarnation through love (this seems to be the purpose in the emphasis on

---

[9]There is, however, mythological precedent for the interpenetration of mortal and god; in an earlier Hittite story, the god Telepinus becomes enraged and disappears; both Earth and Heaven are affected. On Earth, grain ceases to grow and animals to breed; in heaven, the gods "ate, but did not quench their thirst" (Pritchard, V.1, p. 87). It is a mortal whose worship and appeal are able to effect change in Telepinus, where the pleas of the other gods fail to move him. In the myth, though, it is *worship* of the divine by the mortal, evidence of dependence, which causes change, rather than a bond between the two based on mutual desire.

Cupid's pain at the burn); and for the purposes of divine order, it is necessary for that grounding to take place.

PSYCHIC ORDERING PRINCIPLES AND THEIR INTERRELATIONS

Confronted by the admonitions of Ceres and Juno, Venus retreats to the open sea: she represents an oceanic principle of eros while Jove represents an ordering, ruling principle of logos. Both Cupid and Psyche derive from the principle represented by Venus. In order for Cupid and Psyche to unite and produce a new *coniunctio*, Venus's eros-disseminating energy must interact with Jove's more ordering quality.

Venus's servants torture Psyche; afterwards, Venus begins to assign her tasks. In the first task, the sorting of seeds, a compassionate ant exhorts the other "nimble, all-producing foster-daughters of the earth" (*miseremini terrae omniparentis agiles alumnae*) to help Psyche. The word *alumnae*, meaning nursling, foster-child, pupil, is actually an adjective used as a noun, so its gender may change. Here, Apuleius, by using the feminine gender to designate that the ants are foster-*daughters* of the Earth, implies an innate archetypal organizing principle manifesting through the Earth and comprising a unifying force through the harmonious working together of the multiplicity of cells in this body, rather than the overarching, rational structuring of solar consciousness.

In the second task, Psyche must gather wool from the rams, who represent a dangerous aspect of solar consciousness. This requires mediation from a reed, which cautions Psyche to gather the wool from bushes after the strongest rays of the sun have faded.

In Latin, the reed, *arundo viridis* (a green reed), is then modified further by the phrase *de fluvio musicae suavis nutricula*, nurse of sweet music from the river. More telling than the feminine gender of the word *nutricula* is the fact that the word means nourisher, a specifically feminine term, as its root is nutrix, which means wet nurse. Thus, the reed represents wisdom that stems from nourishment.

We see unmediated solar elements in patients' impulses to speak or act out. For example, in sessions John would spiral into great angers, becoming louder and louder, as he relived the difficult interactions of his week. As he became more manic in his rage, however, I noticed that I was feeling very sad. Finally, my eyes filled with tears as the depression lying under the rage became pronouncedly projected into me. John's split-off lunar elements entered my psyche and my body. This sorrow was not sorrow *for* him so much as *his sorrow*, carried by me. This process helped stimulate John's split-off lunar elements to enhance a sorely needed capacity for reflection.

The lack of lunar elements and the dominance of the dangerous solar elements can also be seen with patients who, lacking the capacity to sit with their feelings long enough to contain them, feel the urgent necessity of jumping in with words. This latter dynamic is not limited to the patient: as analysts, one of the most difficult tasks is sitting with the pain and horror of the patient's emptiness and despair. Although our conscious reasons for speaking are to end the pain in which the patient sits, the unconscious reasons have more to do with our anxiety aroused by their pain.

One important amplification of the reed connects it to Syrinx, a nymph whom Pan tried to rape. She fled and when she could run no more, Syrinx begged her "sisters of the stream" to turn her into a reed (Ovid, I, 705). From these reeds Pan made his flute, saying, "This converse at least shall I have with thee" (I, 710). The Pan/Syrinx story demonstrates a failed attempt at handling the fiery masculine principle so as to make it accessible to the ego.

The solar/lunar elements' activity represents an interactive, dynamic system. It is not simply a matter of solar elements being dangerous for women: rather both elements are necessary for a well-functioning ego state. Each alone can be dangerous: thus, Pan represents a danger for Echo and Syrinx, a raw, primitive energy—but Echo and Syrinx represent an energy out of the reach of Pan. The experience of the reed saves Psyche by mediating this too violent symbol of consciousness with the cool, reflective inwardness of lunar consciousness; Syrinx herself could only run, metamorphosing into vegetative life. Still, she retains a voice, a means to place her wisdom at Psyche's disposal.

The third task necessitates the retrieval of water from the source for the rivers Styx and Cocytus. Neumann says that "the essential feature of this spring is that it connects the highest and the lowest . . . the essential quality of this stream is precisely that it cannot be contained" (1956, p. 103). Psyche cannot contain the water herself, as is overemphasized in the text by the list of horrors and difficulties in her way.

This time the mediating figure is an aspect of Jove as an eagle, an instinctual aspect of the ruling principle. The presence of this "rescuer" hints that the story is about an individuation plan, since Jove represents an overarching structure of order within which Psyche's process can procede. Although the water is declared to be dreaded, the eagle succeeds by pretending he is sent by Venus. Perhaps Venusian powers can overcome death. Also, the text emphasizes that the container, given to Psyche by Venus, is a vessel made of smoothed or inlaid crystal (*crystallo dedolatum vasculum*), not a magical container. The energy of Venus *plus* the mediating energy of the eagle allows the water to be contained by Psyche.

Venus gives Psyche one last task: to ask Proserpina, Queen of Hades, to fill a box with a small amount of beauty for Venus. Once again, Psyche feels despair and seeks to end her life, this time by throwing herself from a tower. But the tower warns her not to separate her spirit from her body, giving her directions to avoid dangers in her path in the underworld.

By warning Psyche to "beware of pressing forward unprovisioned into these caverns of darkness" (Apuleius 1932, p. 138), the tower is imparting information regarding necessary safeguards for entrance into the unconscious. There are the sops to Cerberus, a kind of homeopathic remedy used to quiet the ferociousness of the unconscious, as the soaking of the cakes in wine implies a dose of chaos; another is the coins for Charon.

In therapy, payment can become a leitmotif of complaining energy; analysts can feel persecuted by the recurrence of this thread in sessions with a patient. An archetypal foundation exists, however, that underlies all such interactions and can provide a way to view this as a serious psychological occurrence, not avoided or taken only as a manifestation of a transferential derivative about the specific analytic interaction. Von Franz calls Charon "a personification of . . . 'the transcendent function' . . . in that it transcends our conscious grasp and . . . enables men to pass from one psychic state to another" (1980, p. 100).

If, as Jung says, the "transcendent function arises from the union of conscious and unconscious contents" (1946, par. 131), then Psyche *must* enter these depths. Charon's function can be understood as a means of bringing these opposites together, while insisting on the preservation of a ritual structure of readiness to descend. The tower also says, "neither Charon nor the great god Dis, his father, does anything unfee'd" (Apuleius 1932, p. 138), implying an active principle of equivalency. In the context of therapy, the fee must be demanded by the therapist in order to ensure that the patient is both prepared for and desirous of the journey.

The tower warns Psyche not to pay attention to requests for help from a lame man with a lame ass, or the piteous cries of the corpse of an old man in the river, because pity is unlawful. Neumann (1956) and von Franz (1980) speak to the undermining effect of boundless compassion in a woman, and von Franz and Ulanov (1971) relate it to the man's anima. However, these manifold injunctions to Psyche and particularly the warning against pity are connected to a more profound task.

Psyche has immense trouble placing her own interests first. This is why, for example, it would be so wrong for her to follow Pan's advice. She needs to give priority to her own desires. Although we are perhaps more accustomed to thinking of this as a woman's problem (martyr syndrome), for many male patients it takes a slightly different but just as undermining form. One patient felt compelled to be seen as Mr. Good Person and to that end overtipped in cabs and restaurants and continually apologized to everyone whose services he required (e.g., waiters, salespeople). The need to be seen as good dominated his life and compensated for a deep inner conviction that he was intrinsically bad.

The tower also warns Psyche not to join certain old women in their weaving. The word in the text is *textrices*; the related adjective, *textorius*, figuratively means entanglement. Psyche must be careful not to become entangled in their web, and the tower cautions against losing a sop for Cerberus: weaving, which would require both of her hands, could make her drop one. If this happened, she would have no way to soothe Cerberus and would be trapped in Hades forever.

Psychologically this informs us about the ego's ability to stay intact when it enters the realm of the unconscious; the aim of safe return must not be forgotten in the seduction of and fascination with the fate-composing role of the archetypes. These old women (*ani*) have been related to the Fates (Lewis and Short 1879, p. 134) who in turn are related to the Furies (Hesiod, 95 and 95n, 237). The Fates represent a goundplan that supersedes the conscious interests of men or the uncontained desires of gods, and to which each is bound. The only striving may be for one's own path, not for the purpose of changing Fate, but for the purpose of removing impediment to the working out of one's intended plan.

Psyche next enters the mansion of Proserpina where she "refused the seat of ease and the morsel of luxury" (Apuleius 1932, p. 139). The tower had warned Psyche not to eat the luxurious foods Proserpina would offer–but perhaps she also remembers her first encounter with unearned ease and luxury, in her paradise with her invisible husband. Embracing unconsciousness here does constitute ego-death, for those who eat in Hades are doomed to stay. Here, Psyche eats only a humble crust of brown bread which represents the numinosity of the ordinary, containing a grounding quality that links Psyche to earthly life.

The box is secretly filled, sealed, and given to her. She returns to the surface, where she disobeys the tower, who has said, "Above all things, have a regard that thou look not in the box, neither be not too curious about the box of divine beauty" (Apuleius 1566, p. 277). Psyche, however, feels moved to open the box and take a bit for herself, in order to look more beautiful for Cupid. When she does, she finds that,

> it held no Recipe of Beauty. In it lurked Sleep of the Innermost Darkness, the night of Styx, which freed from its cell rushed upon her and penetrated her whole body with a heavy cloud of unconsciousness . . . she collapsed doubled upon the ground; and there she lay without the slightest stir, a corpse asleep. (Apuleius 1932, p. 140)

EMERGENCE OF NEW EGO STRUCTURE

In Robert Browning's words, "a man's reach should exceed his grasp, or what's a heaven for?" and Psyche's action in reaching for a bit of the divine by opening the beauty box represents a death of an old attitude of despair and hopelessness.

Cupid then returns to Psyche, no longer able to bear their separation. He "delicately purg[ed] her of the Sleep, which he put back in its original lair the box, . . . [and] roused Psyche with a charming prick of the arrow" (Apuleius 1932, p. 140). Cupid has developed from a mischievous, dangerous, and untouched boy to a committed lover. His development speaks to the capacity of the individual not only to change on the personal unconscious level, but to change in a fundamental way on the archetypal level.

This can often be seen first in the dreams of patients. Not only can a different image emerge but the same archetype can take profoundly different shapes. When Sam, a successful writer in his thirties, first came into therapy, one of the problems was impotence. Physical impotence was a metaphor for his entire relational life and his depotentiation affected his work as well. A full-length book with which he had been struggling for years remained unfinished.

In the beginning, our work often felt draining. All of the energy in the room seemed to be sucked out. Sam had a recurring dream in therapy: he would be fishing and get a bite on the line; when he reeled it in, he found a dog, which he would then throw back in disgust.

The strain of bearing with his process prevented me from seeing that, incrementally, change was taking place, until the following dream ended the recurring series and revealed the changes happening in his psyche. He dreamed:

> *I was fishing and there was a bite on the line; when I reeled it in, it was a dog. Its hair was black, wet and matted, and it had a spear wound in its side. I felt very sad for it. I decided not to throw it back, but to take it to the vet. While I hurried to get it to the office, the wound healed; now the dog was a golden cocker spaniel. I realized, "This dog doesn't need a vet," decided that I loved it, wanted to keep it, and took it home.*

The dreamer's vision allows him to "see" and feel touched by the dog's suffering. The wound in the side connects the image to Christ, who was also wounded in the side by the spear of the centurion. If Christ could be wounded, bleed, yet be resurrected after death, then the dream is indicating a piece of the patient's psyche that can be resurrected, transformed.

When Sam was a little boy, his parents often showed him pictures of a cocker spaniel they had when they married; they spoke fondly of this dog and their love for it. For Sam, this represented an early, golden time when eros still existed between his parents, eros which had disappeared by the time he was born.

This dream indicates the breaking up of the black, bloody, and wounded internal couple, where the instinctual energy was blocked and drained out of Sam's inner being and outer life. The archetype represented by "dog" had evolved: in the black was found the gold and Sam's eros had now the potential to be found and liberated.

Psyche, too, manifests significant change: she expresses a wish to be more beautiful – a normal wish for a girl in love, but one she could not have made before, when her beauty represented her unconsciousness. The ambivalence of the divine places into the hands of the ego the possibility of becoming a new third identity combining ego and Self. Psyche reaches for the contents of the box not to steal, but to use some small bit (*Quae nec tantillum quidem indidem mihi delibo*), with the intention of returning it to Venus. As instructed by Cupid, "Psyche brought back to Venus the gift of Proserpina," (Apuleius 1566, p. 278) (*Psyche vero confestim Veneri munus reportat Proserpinae*).[10] In his essay, "On the Nature of the Unconscious," Jung comments:

> Conscious wholeness consists in a successful union of ego and self, so that both preserve their intrinsic qualities. If, instead of this union, the ego is overpowered by the self, then the self too does not attain the form it ought to have. (1946, par. 430n)

This sequence in the tale relates to the ego's now-balanced connection to the Self. Artists know the feeling of having an inner vision that remains perfect only when not separated from the Self and manifested by the ego.

It is not only the artist who fears the impossibility of communicating a vision intact. For a person who enters analysis embedded in the Self, inner realities feel violated in the attempt to communicate them in analysis. The imperfection of human expression compared to the inner reality of a sacred vision feels painful and humiliating to demonstrate to another. Traumas expressed through these states of being stem from damage at a preverbal level, where the earliest feelings of oneness with the mother may have been damaged before the ability to speak was developed.

Patients in this state may sleep much of the time, not to escape but to safely contact a realm that otherwise can feel overwhelming. This was the psychology of the musician cited earlier: while his music poured forth direct from the Self, he had never developed any but the most rudimentary and functional of egos.

---

[10] If Venus's beauty depends on Proserpina, one might speculate whether, as Wallace Stevens says, "Death is the mother of beauty."

Dante, in the first canto of the *Paradiso*, sends up a prayer to Apollo asking for help in writing his recollections of Paradise, saying "I saw things that he/who from that height descends, forgets or can/not speak" (*Paradiso*, I, 5–7). He recognizes that "passing beyond the human cannot be worded" (*Paradiso*, I, 70), that the expression of his transcendent vision will need mediation from this particular facet of the godhead in order to find adequate expression back on Earth.

The heavy sleep that overcomes Psyche is like death. Sleep and death are connected mythologically. Marcus Cornelius Fronto, telling how Jove created sleep, states that the gods rejoice in activities of the night. Jupiter, however, decides that the night cannot be left as a realm within which man stays awake to be manipulated by the gods. He therefore created Sleep,

> and enrolled him among the gods, set him in charge over night . . . [and] mixed with his own hands the juice of herbs . . . of security and delight . . . from the groves of Heaven but the herb of death was sought in the meadows of Acheron. Of that death, he mingled but one drop and that the tiniest, as is the tear of one who would hide his tears. (Fronto, II, 17)

Jove then committed to sleep a "death" from which mankind could awake, along with a "multitude of blissful dreams" (ibid.).[11]

Dreams are the bridge between the conscious and unconscious, often the first place where psychological change manifests, before the waking ego experiences it. Self and ego, archetypal and material events mingle freely. Asleep, we have no volition and are vulnerable to the power of the unconscious and its language of symbols.

INCARNATING NEW ENERGY

After he rescues Psyche, the active role in the tale shifts to Cupid. He pleads with Jove to legalize their marriage, and Jove acquiesces, calling the gods together to declare,

---

[11]The "Creation of Sleep" appears in a long letter from Fronto, a great correspondent and royal tutor, to his pupil, Marcus Aurelius. Written in 162 A.D., it is thought by some to have influenced Apuleius, an influence which can be seen most clearly in the beauty box episode in "Cupid and Psyche."

> I have deemed it advisable to restrain the heated impulses of his young blood by some means or other. No further reasons need be adduced than the daily scandals he creates. . . . all occasion for this must be removed, and his youthful sportiveness must be hampered with nuptial fetters. He has chosen a girl and seduced her. Let him take her and possess her . . . I shall legislate that the marriage is not a misalliance but perfectly in accord with usage and the civil code. (Apuleius 1932, p. 141)

Psychologically, the union of Cupid and Psyche grounds the unrestrained energy represented by Cupid, producing a third principle in the psyche, reflected by the birth of their child, a girl named Voluptas.

Apuleius often uses the word *voluptas* in his novel. There are other words for pleasure in Latin such as *delectatio, libido,* and *oblectamentum,* but these words define functions, meaning diverting, amusing, a pastime. *Voluptas* is a word defining a *state of being.* A closer look at the roots of the meaning of the words involved in this tale illuminates the state of being.

Cupid comes from the word *cupidus,* which means desire, wish, longing; *cupio,* the verb form, derives from the Sanskrit *kup* and designates a natural, involuntary inclination or an unbridled or passionate desire, which describes quite well the movement of archetypal forces. The root word for *Voluptas* is *volo,* to wish, intend, purpose, propose, consent—words that indicate an energetic will, a more human quality.

Cupio represents an energy with its own movement independent of ego. The feelings of greed, envy, or obsessive love come under this category. The Greek root for *volo* is the verb meaning to hope, also a human energy. The archetypal realm may carry the ingredients for hope but does not itself embody hope; it simply is, in its inchoate being.

Cupid and Psyche represent pairs of opposites: male/female, human/archetypal, inchoate urge/purposeful soul. They flee from one another yet are linked through desire. It is through their union that the child Voluptas is produced. As Jung says, "Although the opposites flee from one another, they nevertheless strive for balance, since a state of conflict is too inimical of life to be endured indefinitely" (1955, par. 307).

Voluptas represents the suppressed feminine element which was eclipsed as the patriarchal era gathered momentum. Unlike Venus, she contains and connects earth/moon consciousness with the solar realm. Just as the old energies go into eclipse, she promises the possibility of a consciousness that is rooted in the senses but linked to illumination.

This is not a return of the goddess in the sense of the original undifferentiated energy represented by Venus. Instead, the archetype "goddess" has evolved to include solar/lunar, masculine/feminine, human/divine elements. The return of this suppressed and feared energy in the psyche was promised two thousand years ago, just as another great event in human history was seizing Western consciousness; this evolved energy constitutes a missing healing element that can now be integrated and join two realms of consciousness.

REFERENCES

Alighieri, D. *The Divine Comedy: Paradiso*. Translated by Allen Mandelbaum. 1984. New York: Bantam.

Apuleius. 1566. *The Golden Ass: Being the Metamorphoses of Lucius Apuleius*. W. Adlington, trans. S. Gaselee, ed. Cambridge, Mass.: Harvard University Press, 1915.

Apuleius. 1932. *The Golden Ass*. Jack Lindsay, trans. Bloomington, Ind.: Indiana University Press, 1962.

Balint, M. 1968. *The Basic Fault: Therapeutic Aspects of Regression*. New York: Brunner/Mazel, 1979.

De Rougement, D. 1983. *Love in the Western World*. M. Belgion, trans. Princeton, N.J.: Princeton University Press.

Durand, G. 1981. Psyche's view. J. A. Pratt, trans. *Spring*, 1981:1–19.

Fordham, M. 1965. The importance of analysing childhood for assimilation of the shadow. *Journal of Analytical Psychology* 10/1:33–47.

Fronto, M. C. 1919. *The Correspondence of Marcus Cornelius Fronto*. C. R. Haines, trans. Cambridge, Mass.: Harvard University Press.

Hesiod. *The Homeric Hymns and Homerica*. H. G. Evelyn-White, trans. Cambridge, Mass.: Harvard University Press, 1914.

Hieatt, A. K., and Park, W. 1972. *The College Anthology of British and American Poetry*. Boston: Allyn and Bacon.

Hillman, J. 1972. *The Myth of Analysis*. Evanston, Ill.: Northwestern University Press.

Hubback, J. 1972. Envy and the shadow. *Journal of Analytical Psychology* 17/2:152–165.

Jung, C. G. 1946. On the nature of the psyche. In *Collected Works* 8:159–234. Princeton, N.J.: Princeton University Press, 1960.

______. 1948. *Aion: Researches into the Phenomonology of the Self*. In *Collected Works*, vol. 9/2. Princeton, N.J.: Princeton University Press, 1960.

———. 1952. *Symbols of Transformation*. In *Collected Works*, vol. 5. Princeton, N.J.: Princeton University Press, 1956.

———. 1955. *Mysterium Coniunctionis*. In *Collected Works*, vol. 14. Princeton, N.J.: Princeton University Press, 1970.

———. 1959. Good and evil in analytical psychology. In *Collected Works* 10:456–468. Princeton, N.J.: Princeton University Press, 1964.

Lewis, C. T., and Short, C. 1879. *A Latin Dictionary*. Oxford: Clarendon Press, 1982.

Longus. *Daphnis and Chloe*. G. Thornley, trans. J. M. Edmonds, ed. Cambridge, Mass.: Harvard University Press, 1916.

Nonnos. *Dionysiaca*. W. H. D. Rouse, trans. Cambridge, Mass.: Harvard University Press, 1940.

Neumann, E. 1956. *Amor and Psyche, The Psychic Development of the Feminine: A Commentary on the Tale by Apuleius*. R. Mannheim, trans. New York: Pantheon.

Ovid. *Metamorphoses*. F. J. Miller, trans. Cambridge, Mass.: Harvard University Press, 1916.

Pritchard, J. B., ed. 1958. *The Ancient Near East: An Anthology of Text and Pictures*. Princeton, N.J.: Princeton University Press.

Roscher, W. H. 1884–1886. *Ausfurliches Lexicon der Greichischen und Romischen Mythologie, vol. 1*. Leipzig: Teubner.

Rose, H. J. 1959. *A Handbook of Greek Mythology, Including Its Extension to Rome*. New York: E. P. Dutton and Co.

Schwartz-Salant, N. 1982. *Narcissism and Character Transformation: The Psychology of Narcissistic Character Disorders*. Toronto: Inner City Books.

Stevens, W. 1959. *Poems*. New York: Vintage.

Ulanov, A. 1971. *The Feminine in Jungian Psychology and in Christian Theology*. Evanston, Ill.: Northwestern University Press.

Winkler, J. 1985. *Auctor and Author: A Narratological Reading of Apuleius' Golden Ass*. Berkeley: University of California Press.

"*The Dark Man's Sooty Brother*"
Male Naivete and the Loss of the Kingdom

Robert Bly

Once upon a time there was a soldier who had just been discharged. While walking in the woods, in that curious mood we feel after having been discharged, he met a man with an odd-shaped foot. "Why are you sad?" "I don't know what to do next." "You could work for me." "What is the work?" "You would live underground at my place and spend seven years working for me. Then you're free. During that time, you cannot comb your hair, nor wash, nor cut your fingernails or your toenails nor your beard, nor wipe the tears from your eyes."

So he went with the man who took him underground and showed him the three pots. "You'll be tending my three pots and keeping them boiling. You will not look into the pots. Is that clear? And the shavings you will sweep behind the door. Can you do it?"

"I can," he said.

He chopped wood, put the wood chunks under the huge, black, covered pots, kept the fires going, and swept the shavings behind the door. After three or four months, he said to himself, "I think I'll peek into the first pot." He did, and to his surprise he saw his sergeant sitting there. "Oh ho!" he said. "You had me in your power, but now I have you in my power." And he added more wood to that fire. He worked a few more months and then felt the desire to peek into the second pot. He did and saw his lieutenant sitting there. "Ah ha!" he said. "You once had me in your power, but now I have you in my power." And he added a lot more wood to that fire. Six months or so later, he couldn't resist his longing to peek into the third pot. He lifted the cover and who did he see but his old general–General Westmoreland!–sitting in that pot. "Well, well!" he said. "Once you had me in your power, but now I have you in my power." He chopped extra wood and added good dry oak under that pot.

When the Dark Man returned to see how the work was going, he remarked, "By the way, you looked into the pots, and if you hadn't added more wood, I really would have punished you."

Time seemed to pass faster now, what with the extra chopping each day, and week by week the time went by, and the seven years were up.

The Dark Man returned and said, "You've done your work well." He swept up some of the shavings behind the door, put them in a gunny sack, gave the sack to the man, and said, "Here are your wages." The man was disappointed, but what can you do? Always remember to arrange your wages beforehand. The Dark One said: "When anyone asks you where you have come from, you say, 'From under the earth.' If they ask who you are, you are to say, 'I am the Dark Man's Sooty Brother and my King as well.' " It didn't really make sense, but he memorized the sentence and prepared to go back to the world.

He left the workplace and the strangest thing was this: as he made his way up to our world, the shavings in his bag all turned to gold. That pleased him, of course. Eventually he came to an inn and asked for a room. "Where do you come from?" asked the innkeeper. "From under the earth." "Who are you?" "I am the Dark Man's Sooty Brother and my King as well." He hadn't shaved for seven years, nor wiped the tears from his eyes–you remember that–so the innkeeper did not find him to be an appetizing guest and said, "I'm sorry, but I have no rooms left for tonight." Then this worker made his first mistake–he opened the sack and showed the innkeeper his gold. The innkeeper now said, "Well, as I think of it, I remember that my brother, who has been in #10, is going away this weekend, and you can have his room tonight." So it was. In the middle of the night the innkeeper crept into the room and stole the gold. Our friend felt bad about it, but he said to himself: "It was through no fault of mine," and decided to go back underground.

He found the Dark Man, told him what happened and what he wanted. The Dark Man said, "Sit down. I'll wash you now and comb your hair, and cut your nails and beard, and wipe your eyes." When that was done, the Dark Man gave him a second bag of shavings and said, "Tell the innkeeper you want your gold back. If he doesn't do it, he'll have to come here and take your place. I will come for him." So Hans told the innkeeper that and reminded him that if he went down, he would end up looking just like Hans did. That was enough; the innkeeper gave him the money back and more. So Hans was rich now.

He started off to see his father, bought a white coat of coarse cloth, and made a living travelling around the country and performing music on an instrument he had learned to play while underground. Eventually, the king of that country heard his music and offered Hans his oldest daughter. When she saw the quality of his coat, she said, "I'd prefer to jump in the river." So, he married the youngest daughter and got half the kingdom. When the king died, Hans inherited the entire kingdom. That was luck. As for storytellers, we still wander around with holes in our shoes.

We've heard a fairy story, or as Shakespeare called such stories, "A Winter's Tale," about a male descent into the underworld from which the youth retrieves some gold shavings; he later loses them in his naiveté and unprotection to a false innkeeper. He passively allows the innkeeper to steal his gold because he is asleep at the time. So naiveté and passivity relate to a kind of sleep. In naiveté, one is asleep to the greed, ill motives, and shadow side of oneself and of others; in passivity, one is asleep to the daytime activities of alertness and expressiveness; when the chest is asleep, the heart is asleep. Naiveté, passivity, and numbness are not male diseases, but in contemporary culture they seem a deepening danger to men.

This story begins well with the lostness and the conversation with the strange-footed man. The job underground embodies the old mythological theme of the underworld and suggests some form of initiation for young men, guided by an old earth type. In Grimm, the story is named "The Devil's Sooty Brother," but one needn't pay too much attention to the word "devil." I would guess it was added in Christian times to a tale already thousands of years old. The being is probably some old earth god of northern Europe—we remember Pan's goat feet. A sculpture of the wild man built into a Spanish cathedral of the Middle Ages shows him with one animal foot. So we could call this underworld being a "dark man," a relative of the Wild Man. It is interesting that the young man who descends with him is required to retain some characteristics of the Wild Man—long hair, uncut nails, and unconcealed grief. He agrees "not to wipe the tears from his eyes."

He agrees to go underground. That is the most important detail in the story. Sometimes a man will embark on "men's work" but refuse to go underground. Men of this sort become consumers of myths, connoisseurs of fairy tales, judges of the conference leaders, playboys of growth.

To go underground is to go into Hades. The dark men one meets there may not be, as James Hillman says in *The Dream and the Underworld*, symbols of virility but messengers of death.

> Perhaps they are the horses of that heathen Attila
> or the black messengers sent to us by death.
>
> Vallejo

To go into the underworld is to go into eclipse. A shadow moves across the moon woman, whose circle lights the waters, and the shadow thrown by the very earth we live on overwhelms the circle. The animals and birds normally making sound in moonlight fall silent. Baboons howl in nervousness. This underworld state can go on for years. This is a Winter's Tale.

The Descender's job is to keep three kettles boiling. For that he has to chop wood, but strangely the shavings turn out to be important. The Dark Man's instructions are precise: sweep the shavings behind the door. If we try that, we find that when we open the door to let our friends or enemies in, the shavings will not be visible, for the opened door will hide them; but when the visitors leave and we close the door once more, all these shavings will be visible to our own eyes once more. So the story recommends a beautiful little dance of hiding and revealing. The Iron John story urges the young man to hide his gold; here he is to hide the shavings as well.

What are these shavings? We know that certain insights come only when we are depressed. If we go down in order to bring up a poem, let's say, certain lines will get written and then thrown away, and therapy when done well produces many pre-thoughts and afterthoughts. Certain ideas about our life which we come upon, say in therapy, don't seem to amount to much at the time—but when we come back up into "our world" these insignificant ideas turn to gold. That's good to know.

And this chopping one does when "underground"–what's the point of it? To keep the pots boiling, our story says. The shavings are an extra gift. To his surprise, the fire-tender finds people sitting in the pots! It turns out that our old sergeants, lieutenants, and generals have come to sit down in those pots. We should remind ourselves that there are no people in a fairy story, so no person is being boiled. These are nonmolecular creatures inside our soul. The first pot holds an image of the sergeant. We could say that it is an image of authority. Some of us might need to glimpse a high school principal there, or a harsh grandmother, or the critic who offered humiliation when we showed our first poems. Usually we sit hunched up beneath these critics, inert, resigned, stuck; so it is a great advance just to get them off our backs, into a pot, sitting in hot water.

Our story says that being passive toward these beings is not the thing–one has to be active toward them, boil them. That requires a "dark man," apparently, an underground place, some pots, chopping, heat, ashes, soot. We notice also that the completion of it requires active disobedience of the first orders the boss gave us.

Apparently, images of the sergeant and other officers change when boiled, as milk changes to cheese. Some trancelike power that the authority figures had gets boiled away. "Once I was in your power; now you are in my power." What is that like in daily life? I would say that to get a hold on the main lines of your father's life would be a boiling. To see which people shamed you in your childhood and how they did it, and who in this place continues to shame you would be a boiling. Power works on us namelessly when we are children; as adults our job is to name it. That in itself helps get rid of naiveté and encourages shrewdness to develop. When the young man looks in the pots and piles wood on the fire, he is doing well. When he is about to go back up, the old earth god warns him about the importance of language. When someone asks who he is, he is to say: "I am the Dark Man's sooty brother and my King as well." He is not to say: "I have spent three years at the Jung Institute in Zurich under Marie-Louise von Franz and I am a licensed Jungian therapist," nor "I am a Quaker since birth and now an overseer in my Friends Meeting," nor "I am a young intuitive working on my individuation." Those would be naive answers that would call up inflation in the speaker and an urge to kill in the listeners. He is to say: "I am the Dark Man's sooty brother and my King as well." He isn't the Dark

Man's shiny brother, but the Dark Man's sooty brother, and he is "my King as well." That phrase makes no more sense in German than in English, but it suggests that the process of boiling has freed him from some reliance on outer authority or outer kingship, so that he is, to some extent, his own king. That's very good.

But, alas, when the young man shows his bag of gold ingenuously to the innkeeper, it's clear that he is still a fool, even after the seven years of boiling. This complicated experience hasn't cured his naiveté. The naive quality in young men hangs on. So I think we could profitably spend a little time talking about naiveté.

"Naiveté," according to the dictionary, is "natural simplicity or artlessness; ingenuousness." But looked at from behind, it is a state of feeling that avoids the dark side of one's own motives or the motives of others. Naiveté discounts anger, fear, or greed and assumes more goodness in the world than there is. The naive person often refuses confrontation or combat and, if thrown into combat by circumstance, often fails to notice that he has in fact been defeated. Wearing a white suit, he rides about the field where the defeat took place, waving to the onlookers as if he were the victor.

Naiveté seems to be characteristic of American men in the last forty years; we could say that Hemingway represents a successful fight against it – he tried to see defeat as defeat. But in Kerouac, and the "sixties writers" in general, the fight is lost. At all times in history, men moreover appear to be naive in relationship even when they are relatively shrewd in their worldly dealings.

We've mentioned that the naive man doesn't see his own defeat even when it takes place in front of thousands. He also doesn't notice when an invader crosses his border. He doesn't know "manners." In earlier times in Japan, when a guest arrived at the door, the host would have said something like this: "For a humble and utterly worthless person such as myself, it is an unspeakable honor for my family and all my ancestors to greet the celestial person that you are." He doesn't believe a word of it, but the sentence reminds the other soul and his own of boundaries around both parties. Such sentences prevent inappropriate mergings and make invasion of the psyche less likely. Goethe said:

> Tell a wise person or else keep silent,
> because the mass man will mock it right away.

The naive person doesn't fear the mass man and may idealize him. The naive man at a party will tell utter strangers his most intimate experiences. It was a mass man who invented the Encounter Group. "During this weekend," says the encounter leader, "I want you to get everything out. Don't hold back anything. We want to know how you feel about your mother."

The story says that when you are too naive in your offering, an innkeeper, whom we'll call the false innkeeper, called forth by the naiveté, steals your gold, and he has to. He has no choice. The naive man often puts much emphasis on "sincerity." He feels, for example, that if he tells a person sincerely what he has done, that person should forgive him right away. "It's true I betrayed her, but I did tell her right away. I don't know why she is so angry. I was really frank with her." He thinks his sincerity should protect him from a long look at his shadow side. He enters a tunnel without noticing the tendency of a tunnel to become narrower and darker. "Let's hope for the best." The hopeful way the American politicians entered the tunnel called the Vietnam War was highly naive; and the Russians were equally naive in entering Afghanistan.

During the last few decades, both men and women have begun to love the word "wholeness" even though none of us have ever met anyone who is whole. All this use of the word *wholeness* then, holistic world views, wholeness and healing, whole earth catalog, wholeness newsletter, encourages naiveté and inflames the false innkeeper to outrageous acts of theft. Naiveté, as our story says, works hand in hand with betrayal. The naive man trusts the charismatic leader such as Ronald Reagan, who immediately steals the gold. The naive man trusts his boss and the boss overworks him. His children turn him into a slave, his wife leads him by the nose and recognizes that all he can do is forgive and daydream about wholeness.

Once his gold has been stolen, the young man has lost the payment or reward for all his work. One could say that his therapy has failed; or one could say that he has slipped back into some childhood state of dependency and denial; or if he is an artist, one could say that he has settled for kitsch, a comfortable work of art that ignores "the ugly facts." One could say that his initiation process has gone off track, or that his inward emotional body has not become activated.

We'll look at the latter possibility. I have heard person after person at men's conferences testify that they grew up without any model of what an activated masculine emotional body is. Some men describe scenes in childhood in which the mother flew into a rage, directed at the father or at men in general, and their father said nothing, sank into silence and guilt, or disappeared from the room, having defended neither himself nor the boy. Others have known only robotlike fathers without depth. The man without an activated emotional body may alternate between abusive behavior and impotent gentleness that isn't really gentle. Robert Moore remarked that two distinguishing marks of the uninitiated man are wife beating and the contrary softness.

Sometimes sons will try to activate their own emotional bodies through rock music or gang activity, but it does not succeed. A woman who notices that a man's emotional body is not activated will sometimes offer to activate it for him, by helping him to express his feelings or teaching him to be more sensual. It may be that sex deepens the integration of physical and emotional body in a woman, but the same thing doesn't seem to work for a man. In general, I would say that the emotional body of a man cannot be activated by a woman. That's the job of old men, such as the man in our story. In some cultures, the older men give years and years of their lives to just that.

The old men who still today initiate boys in Australian aborigine tribes in New Guinea and in African tribes take boys away from the mothers between the ages of eight and twelve and begin a complicated sequence of adventures, teachings, trials, and dances. The old men recite poems, act out myths, say outrageous things, and may themselves dance all night. The boys experience close up what the emotional body of a man is like when it is activated. The boys in some African tribes are taught to dance for twenty-four hours straight.

"The Dark Man's Sooty Brother" doesn't go into detail on how the emotional body, once the young man has come up, is activated, but it provides a brilliant image for the second part of the work: "I will go back down." So the young man has to go back "down" a second time. The false innkeeper has stolen his "insights"; the old patterns have returned; all the work has apparently been for nothing. That state of diminishment we all know of. The proper response, the story says, is not resignation, beer-drinking, season tickets to the Bears, more talks on male mythology, but rather: "I'll go back down."

All the details are fascinating in this part of the story. We know that the young man agreed not to cut his hair or his fingernails when he took the job, and he kept that promise; but when the seven years are up, the young man says nothing about any obligations the Dark Man has in that area. The kettle-keeper goes back up with his hair still uncut, his fingernails long, etc. Inertness in the emotional body shows itself in failing to ask others for what we want and what we deserve. The young man is too agreeable, too helpful; one could say he keeps on giving to those parts of the psyche that are insatiable. A wife, a boss, a son, a daughter, a guru, can stand in for that clawed part of the soul that eats and is never satisfied.

But when the young man goes down the second time, he says to the Dark Man two things: "Give me some more wages" and "Cut my hair, trim my fingernails, wipe the tears from my eyes, cut my toenails." I love this part; it seems to me so brilliant. Jung remarked: "American marriages are the saddest in all the world, because the man does all his fighting at the office." How difficult it is to say to a wife, "Cut my hair." Instead men live through years of a relationship secretly resentful, dimly enraged, passively hostile. And we are not only talking of marriage here, or agreeabilities in the outer world. Doesn't the dark one inside deserve some orders? Or rather, suppose the Dark Man inside is waiting for an order? We know that the dark ones in the psyche do not act until asked to. Some readers will remember Kafka's story about the doorkeeper and the suppliant. The suppliant waits by the door for months, for years, waiting for the moment the door opens or when the doorkeeper falls asleep, or when he will be invited in. Years pass. Finally when old and dying, he calls the doorkeeper over and whispers to him about the injustice of it all. The doorkeeper say, "Oh this was *your* door; you could have gone through at any moment." And the suppliant dies.

Sociologists report that 48 percent of American men are now employed either by one of the top ten giant corporations or by the United States government. We have to expect that the passivity of which Kafka speaks will deepen. Writers in Eastern Europe, where a characteristic state bureaucracy has been in force for several generations, have described in Kafka-like terms the emotional stagnation, mingling resentment, malice, and shame that results from bureaucratic control. "As Gregor Samsa awoke one morning from uneasy dreams, he found himself transformed in his bed into a gigantic insect" ("Metamorphosis" by Kafka). Fundamentalist religions require a dependent mind. Ollie North's story makes clear that furious and independent activity in one area does not rule out a sheeplike and passive attitude toward higher authority in another.

Disciples in Oregon allow the guru to do all the Rolls Royce owning; devoted traditionalists allow Jimmy Swaggart to have all the biblical interpretations; channelers allow the unearthly spirit invading them to state all his or her opinions without objection or discussion. "I don't have any responsibility; I don't even know what the spirit says, because I'm not here during the channeling." The channeler's audience is equally passive and hears outrageous assertions without asking for evidence. Americans during the last administration acted as if Reagan were a channeler; most citizens agreed with his optimistic opinions on the economy and the poor, even when they had to stumble over the homeless on the sidewalk to get home to watch TV.

We begin to understand now the meaning of the last phrase in the sentence: "I am the Dark Man's sooty brother, and my King as well." Evidence of kingship is the ability to say to the Dark Man in a convincing voice: "Cut my hair." The inner king is the one inside who can decide on one's course for the next six months, the next year, the next twenty years, without being overly contaminated by the ideas of other people on that subject. Our story says kingship also involves telling inner people—who are not kings, warriors or lovers—what you want.

What else can one say about this marvelous story? It turns out that while he was in the underworld, probably his long first period, he learned how to "play music." That is a cunning reference to the emotional body: we remember that Kabir mentioned several times that he often heard music coming from his own chest, even though "no fingers were touching those strings." When we learn how to play a "musical instrument," when the body itself makes music, then a woman hears it, or birds hear it, or other men hear it, or a "king's daughter" hears it. And then this underworld worker, the man earlier "discharged from the army," who later did not "wipe the tears from his eyes," gains "half the kingdom." We should be so lucky.

REFERENCES

Bly, Robert, trans. 1971. *Neruda Vallejo: Selected Poems*. Boston: Beacon.

Hillman, James. *The Dream and the Underworld*. New York: Harper and Row.

"The Fisherman and His Wife" The Anima in the Narcissistic Character

Lionel Corbett
Cathy Rives

Traditional descriptions of the negative anima and animus are uncannily similar to current delineations of narcissistic character pathology. According to Jung, anima and animus are psychological functions that behave like autonomous personalities because they are unconscious, undeveloped, and unintegrated (1928, par. 330). Jung describes the "anima possessed" man as "touchy, irritable, moody, jealous, vain" (1954b, par. 144) or "fickle, capricious . . . uncontrolled and emotional. . . . ruthless, malicious, untruthful, bitchy" (1950, par. 223). The negative animus is said to produce a woman who is "obstinate, harping on principles, laying down the law, dogmatic, world-reforming, theoretical, word-mongering, argumentative, and domineering" (ibid.). Narcissistic character pathology is also characterized by the presence of split-off, often autonomous aspects of the personality, poorly integrated into the individual's fragile self structure, producing moodiness, irritability, grandiosity, and other qualities described by Jung as resulting from the negative animus or anima. Importantly, all of these characteristics can be seen in both men and women.

The tale of the fisherman and his wife aptly depicts one way in which the anima functions within the narcissistic character disorder. It illustrates how a defect in the structures of the per-

sonal self is associated with anima pathology and how the anima may lead to the potential for the transformation of narcissistic structures.

The Fisherman and His Wife

Once a fisherman lived with his wife in a pigsty, and every day he fished in the sea. One day his line was seized, and when he drew it up, he had brought out a large flounder.[1] The flounder said to him, "Please let me live. I am not a flounder, but an enchanted prince. It would do you no good to kill me, and I would not be good to eat, so let me go." The fisherman declared that he would certainly let go of a fish that could talk and let him back into the water. The flounder left a long streak of blood on his way back into the bottom of the sea. When the fisherman told his wife what had happened, she remonstrated with him because he did not make a wish and insisted that the man go back to the flounder and ask for a little hut. Although unwilling, the man was unable to say no to his wife and so went back to the sea. The sea was now no longer clear, but rather green and yellow. The flounder, on hearing the request, immediately granted it.

When the man returned home, he found that he and his wife were living in a nicely decorated little hut with a fine garden. However, this state of contentment only lasted a week or two, at which point the wife insisted that she was not satisfied, because the hut was too small, and that the fisherman should demand from the flounder a great stone castle. Again, the man was unwilling, but unable to say no to his wife. Now, when he came to the sea, the water was purple, dark blue, grey and thick, but still quiet. He passed on to the flounder his wife's request and again the flounder granted her wish.

When he went home, he found an enormous stone palace with a luxurious interior and many servants. There were huge amounts of gold and crystal, beautiful stables, a garden for the animals, and so on. The next morning, however, the wife woke up dissatisfied and insisted that this was not enough, saying, "Couldn't we be the king?" She insisted that he go to the flounder and demand this.

---

[1]It is noteworthy that translators and editors of this story usually retain the capital "F" when referring to the Fisherman and the Flounder. – Corbett

Again, the fisherman argued and the wife said that if he would not be king, then she would be king. He did not wish to go back to the fish, but did so. The sea was now dark grey and the water was heaving and smelled putrid. He stood by it and passed on to the flounder his wife's demand to be king, which was immediately granted.

On his return, the castle had become much larger and was full of servants and an outrageous degree of luxury, and his wife was sitting on an enormous gold throne, surrounded by jewels. The fisherman begged his wife to let things be and wish for nothing more, but she said that time was passing too heavily and she wanted to be emperor as well. The fisherman pleaded with his wife that this was not possible, that it was a shameless request, but the woman imperiously ordered him to go back to the flounder because she was the king and he was nothing but her husband. And so, he was forced to go, although enormously troubled. He went to the sea which was now black, thick and boiling, and a tremendous wind was blowing. He was very afraid but still passed on her request to the flounder who immediately granted it. On his return, the palace had reached even greater heights of luxury and excess. His wife was now sitting on a two-mile-high gold throne with a three-yard-high golden crown, set with diamonds. The man begged his wife to be content, but she insisted that now she wished to be pope. He was again terrified but unable to refuse her demand. This time, as he approached the sea, there was a high wind and a tremendous storm blowing, although in the midst of it all, there was still a small patch of blue visible in the sky. In despair, he conveyed his wife's request to the flounder who granted it.

On his return, his wife was now the pope and was seated amidst ecclesiastical splendor in a church, surrounded by palaces. Again, he begged her to let well enough alone, but she was still dissatisfied. That night, she was unable to sleep because of the problem of deciding what was left for her to be. She spent a restless night and in the morning, when she saw the sun rise, she realized that she was unable to order the sun and moon to rise and that this was what she wanted. She told the horrified fisherman that she wished to be "as God is." He begged her not to press this request, but she flew into a tremendous rage, screamed and kicked him when he argued with her, insisting that she wanted to be like God. He rushed back to the ocean, but now there was an even more terrible storm blowing, houses and trees were falling, mountains were trembling, the sky was pitch black and the sea had enormous waves. Again, he shouted his request to the flounder, who said, "Go to her and you will find her back in the pigsty." And there they are still living to this day.

INTRODUCTION

In our study of this tale, we consider the fisherman as the hero figure, while his wife can be understood either as an outer woman or as an inner figure, as though the entire drama were his dream. This inner figure is condensed in that she personifies related complexes – aspects of both anima and mother complex, as well as the individual's pathologically split-off, archaic grandiose self, in Kohut's (1971) sense. She is depicted as insatiably demanding, angry, inflated, envious, insensitive, and contemptuous of her husband, so that he is gripped by irresistible, recurrent anima-moods and forced into the despair engendered by his own lack of authority. The fisherman behaves like the wounded, incompletely developed "true self" described by Winnicott (1975, p. 212). He is undemanding, self-effacing, passive, and unable to resist his wife's demands. The flounder is considered to be a theriomorphic representation of the Self, contact with which should allow the child to experience an innate sense of worth and joy, which normally leads to the expression of that healthy, developmentally appropriate "grandiosity" which leads to normal self-esteem. Within the fisherman, the energy of the Self has been repressed or squashed. The flounder as enchanted prince also represents the flattened masculine energy within the fisherman's personality. The wife urges a self–Self connection, albeit in a manner fraught with pain for ego-consciousness. We believe that the tale can be used in two ways. First, it illustrates how Jungian theory interacts with and deepens certain current psychoanalytic theories of narcissism. Second, we will attempt to delineate the mechanism by which repression of contact with the Self interacts with pathologic anima development to produce fragile self structures and enfeebled masculinity.

PSYCHODYNAMIC OVERVIEW

The story illustrates certain aspects of the intrapsychic dynamics and emotional fragility of the narcissistic character disorder as it is understood by personalistic psychodynamic theory. From this viewpoint, the two characters illustrate a typical form of intrapsychic splitting, leading to two levels of personality organization that alternate and compete with each other. When the pathological, grandiose self structure is in the ascendent, here depicted by the wife, the individual feels powerful to the point of omnipotence. This results in a feeling of "hypomanic exaltation" (Grunberger 1971, p. 12). Outer objects are then used merely as extensions of one's own grandiosity—the narcissistic character disorder controls others with no regard for their feelings, but rather uses them to feed its own self-esteem, with an endless need for further narcissistic supplies. Notice the wife's total lack of empathy and her rage and indifference to her husband's needs.

This state of optimism is transient, only lasting as long as the individual is gratified. When this fails, the emptiness supervenes, the individual falls into the opposite extreme. The depression, pain, and fear of the individual's vulnerable self is then experienced, depicted here by the hapless fisherman. During periods when the environment does not offer adequate support for the individual's fragile self-esteem, because of poor relationship to the inner world and lack of inner resources, the person with narcissistic character disorder becomes either depressed or enraged, frustrated and disappointed, full of envy, devaluing himself and whomever disappoints him (Kernberg 1975). The fisherman's wife exhibits (personifies) these emotional states as her precarious inflation begins to fail in its task of maintaining her self-cohesion, and this induces anguish in the fisherman.

The story depicts the cyclical oscillation between periods of successful narcissistic activity, when the personality is relatively compensated because the grandiose self structure is being fed by acclaim and success, and periods when the individual cannot sustain grandiosity and falls into "narcissistic unsuccessfulness" (Giovacchini 1978). During such periods, the individual often withdraws into a state of aloof, grandiose isolation accompanied by "transitional fantasies" of increasing greatness, which help the person to recover and find new sources of narcissistic enhancement (Volkan 1973, p. 351).

ARCHETYPAL INFLUENCES ON PERSONAL SELF DEVELOPMENT

This psychodynamic overview is deepened by an understanding of the archetypal forces that influenced the fisherman's development, as they are imaged in this story. The fish is the key link between consciousness and the archetypal realm. The flounder is a flat fish that lives on the bottom of the sea, repressed or squashed down by the greatest pressure. Thus the fisherman brings up from the unconscious what he flounders on, material that he struggles with clumsily – a mixture of his capacity to blunder and founder. The flounder partakes of fish symbolism in general, which alludes not only to mobile contents of the unconscious but also to the sacramental meals of various religious traditions, as well as the depiction of Christ as a fish in the early church (Jung 1954b, par. 127). The fish symbol is the "bridge between the historical Christ and the psychic nature of man, where the archetype of the Redeemer dwells" (Jung 1951b, par. 285). What the fisherman draws up, therefore, has a sacred and redemptive aspect to it. It is a theriomorphic Self symbol; it is not the Self itself, but a Self-representation in a particular sense. It is an image of the Self in a parlous state whose energy is unavailable to consciousness, deeply squashed. But the fisherman paradoxically must also be seen as an aspect of the Self trying to "make his own nature conscious." Christ is not only the fish but also the fisher (Jung 1954c, par. 174; E. Jung and von Franz 1980, pp. 187–191). The "long streak of blood" suggests the crucifixion of Christ and the blood and water flowing from his lance-wound. The debilitated state of the fisherman and the fish both mirror the relatively unconscious or incompletely incarnated state of the Self described in the story. There is an enormous need for renewal of the Self image; the fisherman is a kind of fisher king of the grail legend. E. Jung and von Franz describe how the grail king's suffering worsens at the time of the new moon, relating his wound to a "dark feminine element" (1980, pp. 200–201). Our fisherman, too, suffers from a poor relationship to the feminine which requires redemption. But the fish also has phallic masculine attributes, and this aspect of the Self is in need of renewal; we are told that the flounder is an enchanted prince. He depicts the fisherman's repressed childhood, princelike nature, his innate sense of importance and self-esteem which were presumably squashed by his parents' responses to him. Potentially, therefore, the prince also represents the renewal of the masculine principle – the king-to-be.

Overall, the flounder is the Self as the divine child within the fisherman, still surviving within his own depths and the source of all the power and grandiosity demanded by the fisherman's wife, so that he is forced to return to it again and again. Jung notes that the fish in alchemical symbolism became a symbol of the lapis – the connection with the child is seen when it is sometimes called *infans, puer,* or *filius philosophorum* (1954c, par. 194). As we become more whole, according to Jung, instead of experiencing the Self as an unconscious fish, the Self should be an inner symbolic experience, corresponding to the assimilation of Christ into the psyche as a "new realization of the divine son," no longer in theriomorphic form. This process corresponds to an increase in consciousness (Jung 1951b, par. 286). Kohut's term "transmuting internalization" attempts to describe this process of assimilation at the personalistic level. One is reminded of various mythologies of the divine child (Jesus, Zeus, Krishna, etc.), who combines relative helplessness with unusual power and the capacity for miraculous deeds, now and in the future. This potential is part of the archetypal basis for Kohut's (1971) notion of archaic infantile grandiosity.

It is significant that the flounder, which we have suggested is an image of the Self, is depicted as masculine. The Self must contain both masculine and feminine components and can manifest itself in either form or as a mixture of both (Corbett 1987). Since it strives to produce wholeness within the empirical personality, it will produce an image to consciousness that tries to complete what is missing. Thus the prince-form is a compensation for a deficient masculine consciousness. The "grandiosity" previously referred to represents the subjective experience of the child as it feels its connection to the power of the Self; apparently, this can be given a gender coloring as necessary, so that the child becomes either a prince or a princess.[2]

Because of the squashed quality of the fish, we infer that our fisherman did not receive the normally expected mirroring of his childhood potential for the experience of the Self, which would have led to normal self-esteem, healthy ambition, an embodied sense of soul, good relationship to the contrasexual (Schwartz-Salant 1982), and a sustaining connection to Self out of which the self differentiates. Hillman (1973) points out that the anima tradi-

---

[2]In Kohut's discussion of the development of a personal self, he only focuses on the poles of idealization and grandiosity. We believe that many other potentials need to be considered, including the contrasexual and same-sex components of the personality. Although interlinked with Kohut's two poles, and with the development of the capacity for object love, the differentiation of gender identity and relationship to the contrasexual are separate lines of development with distinctive origins.

tionally performs the function of mirroring and reflection. Thus the fisherman's early anima development must have been distorted. Here, Jung's concept deepens Kohutian theory. The experience of one's soul being mirrored by mother is the child's first experience of anima, and its lack results not only in narcissistic (self structure) deficits but also poor relation to the contrasexual. As Schwartz-Salant points out, such difficulty leads to a missing capacity for reflection and a grandiose power drive, leading to inflation and emphasis on outer appearances, as we see in the story (1982, p. 40). The mirror function of anima, initially performed by mother, is necessary for the full development of consciousness defined as the capacity for self-reflection. It is also necessary for the development of an inner connection to the Self. The consciousness of the infant is initially merged with the Self and must differentiate a sense of separateness while not losing its capacity for relatedness to the Self. The anima in her mirroring (reflecting) aspect is the crucial instrument for this process to occur successfully.[3]

In a man, the personal self is the carrier of conscious masculinity. Because this was unmirrored, it now is unavailable to him. As Jung says, the mother complex wounds the masculine. The fisherman's mother may have been greedily self-absorbed, so that his early anima development was dominated by a mother complex that insisted on being fed at all costs and inhibited the child's sense of his own authority. Or, his mother may have selectively mirrored (reinforced) his negative qualities—his passivity and inertia. Although Jung distinguishes the anima from the mother herself (1951a, par. 26), "the numinous qualities which make the mother imago so dangerously powerful" derive from the anima. Mother is the first carrier of this factor for the son (ibid., par. 28). Probably because of his mother complex, our fisherman is living out his anima problem, such that instead of being in touch with his own masculine authority, he is subservient to an inflated, narcissistic, demanding feminine image.

However, this demanding anima also functions as a bridge to the Self, repeatedly urging him back to what the Self has to offer, even though the fisherman is terrified because this treasure was forbidden to him in childhood. The anima knows that it is avail-

---

[3]The anima or animus experienced in projection performs selfobject functions in Kohut's sense.

able and relentlessly insists that he claim his true authority. She is here seen in her role as psychopomp (Jung 1944, par. 74; 1955–1956, par. 540) or mediatrix between conscious and unconscious (Jung 1955–1956, par. 715). She wants life to be lived, acting as a demon who prevents stagnation (Jung 1950, par. 56). When the anima acts as a forcible bridge to the unconscious, in the presence of negative complexes, this process is extremely painful. The anima also personifies the unconscious as the "realm of the Mothers" (Jung 1955–1956, par. 714) and here the mother complex contaminates the normal anima function in a manner in which power, greed, and envy rather than love dominate the inner world. The fisherman illustrates how the relationship with the anima is a "test of courage, and ordeal by fire . . . hidden in the dominating power of the mother" (Jung 1950, par. 61). Indeed, she may lead us into insanity, and the fisherman is progressively more terrified as the transformative capacity of the feminine seems to provoke increasing intrapsychic chaos.

To feed the increasing needs of his anima, here possessing him in the form of a grandiose structure personified as a power-hungry, insatiable wife, the true self of the fisherman must return to the source within him, the power of his repressed grandiosity, personified by the flounder. This is enchanted, or complex-bound – that is, it has a possessed, autonomous quality and is not integrated within the totality of the personality or readily available to consciousness. Instead of being a joyful source of self-esteem, ambition, and inner goodness, his connection to the Self, his healthy grandiosity, is squashed. When ambition and self-assertion are thus totally repressed and forbidden, the personality is shy and diffident, as we see in the fisherman's behavior. Contact with this level then leads to a painful flooding of consciousness with unrestrained exhibitionistic energy, the energy of the Self which is felt by the ego as unmanageable and shameful because it was so unacceptable to the individual's parents and is consequently still shadowy and unintegrated. He is terrified of his grandiosity because he is still at some level fused with the Self; because he was not mirrored, he remains undifferentiated, and the power of that merger is overwhelming. The fisherman is reminiscent of an individual whose mother demanded that he act as a narcissistic selfobject for her, subject to her omnipotent control and unable to free himself from her domination. His mother may have made him feel ashamed when he exhibited his princelike nature, so that he was never able to assert himself.

Further, he was probably attacked and envied when his parents sensed that he was in touch with the joy of the Self. He is therefore likely to marry a woman who embodied some aspect of his mother problem, who demands submission and gratification from him, and who continues to depotentiate him.

Narcissistic character pathology implies structural deficits in the personal self, which is incompletely formed. In this case, such deficits include incomplete masculine development as well as problematic anima development. There are four sources of masculinity for the child: the innate or archetypal masculine endowment of the child, identification with his father or other important males, his mother's animus, and cultural influences. Since no details are available, we have to speculate on the origins of the fisherman's wounded masculinity based on two clues – the detail of the pigsty, suggesting a mother problem, and the absence of any mention of masculine imagery other than the enchanted prince. The pigsty evokes scenes of mess and filth, as well as greed and laziness. The pig's association with the Great Mother of many mythologies hints at the origin of the fisherman's problem, in a negative mother complex (eg., Walker 1983, p. 112), a Circe-like field. Perhaps this man grew up either without a father or with a very inadequate father, so that he was dependent on his mother to stimulate and mirror his own archetypal masculine potentials. Assuming that the mother had similar pathology to the wife, which is a common arrangement, we would venture a hypothetical description of his mother's difficulties and the effect they had on the growing boy.

We propose that his mother's animus development was weak and unavailable for the enhancement of her self-esteem so that she felt desperate, powerless, ineffectual, fearful, indecisive, and depressed. Her difficulties were projected onto her son, who was affected in two ways. First, his anima, or his potential for relationship to the feminine, was filled in with a powerful mother complex. Second, his archetypal masculine potential, instead of being mirrored, was squashed, perhaps because of mother's envy or hatred of the masculine or her simple inability to see it within her son, since she had little access to it within herself. He identified with and introjected his mother's weakly formed animus, which he now lives out instead of his authentic masculinity. Because of mother's problems, his job as a child was to supply what she needed to sustain her self-esteem. Now he has to perform exactly this function for his wife, who has the same problem as his mother. He is constantly trying to heal his mother's defect. For his own redemption (freeing the enchanted prince), he needs to develop within himself those qualities of masculinity which are also missing in his wife and mother. His wife's raging demands for power and status are not simply derived from her poor relationship to her animus, but are also "disintegration products" of a fragile, narcissistically vulnerable self with little connection to the contrasexual. When she feels herself helpless and needy, her rage and grandiosity attempt to prevent further disintegration and maintain her connection to her selfobject husband while binding her fears.

THE REPRESSED MASCULINE

The prince is clearly a masculine figure whose energy has been unavailable to the fisherman. The obvious question arises as to the precise nature or quality of this energy. In this essay, we have tended to use the terms *anima* and *animus*, *masculine* and *feminine*, according to traditional Jungian theory, which we recognize is inadequate in some important ways. Because the traditional stereotypes of masculinity and femininity are heavily culturally biased (Jung 1928, pars. 338, 330), the usual descriptive terms are not *necessarily* authentically related to the masculine and feminine principles in nature. Recently, a corrective movement has appeared within the field, exemplified by Whitmont's (1982) clarification of the eros–logos polarity. Typological differences, such as those of thinking and feeling, have further obscured this question as it has been discussed in our classical literature.

In recent years, the precise nature of archetypal masculinity and femininity has been called into question. The traditional view, for instance, found in Jung, that masculinity means "knowing what one wants and doing what is necessary to achieve it" (1927, par. 260) is clearly insufficient. It may be completely arbitrary to assign this potential to archetypal masculinity, since our culture has favored its expression in men. Such a definition also implies that femininity means being indecisive and helpless. In fact, qualities such as passivity and activity have been ascribed to the masculine and the feminine in totally opposite ways in different cultures. For example, in the Hindu tantric tradition, the masculine is passive and the feminine active, while Buddhist tantrism reverses these assignations (Bharati 1975). Such appellations occurred because of the manifest matriarchal and patriarchal bias of these cultures. One may argue that the culture distorts the expression of the archetype, or that the archetype informs the culture; as yet this cannot be definitely decided. Qualities such as assertiveness or receptivity may be present in both the archetypal masculine and feminine, but in different proportions. Or, assertiveness and receptivity may be supraordinate factors in which masculinity and femininity are balanced. This would accord with the Taoist view that everything in nature consists of both yin and yang to varying degrees. In other words, assertiveness and receptivity, rather than being exclusively either masculine or feminine, each have yinlike and yanglike properties.

Both characters in the story are suffering from lack of connection to authentic power, authority, self-esteem, and discrimination. These qualities may all be the product of a good self–Self axis and conceivably might have nothing to do with masculinity or femininity. We have also speculated that the fisherman's parents suffered from these difficulties; we have attributed these problems in the female figure to poor animus development and in the man to poor masculine self development, because the story provides this imagery. But the story itself may be culturally biased in its expression of these archetypes. In Gunther Grass's (1978) novel, *The Flounder*, based on this tale, Grass has the storyteller provide two versions, both of which she insists are true. In one version, the fisherman himself carries all the negative qualities of the wife in the Grimms' version. He wants to be unconquerable in war, to accomplish fantastic feats of strength, attain amazing powers, rule the world, subjugate nature, reach for the stars . . . until eventually his whole fantasy collapses into another ice age. Grass uses this device to state a feminist moral, namely, that "all masculine striving leads to chaos." This version of the story is said by Grass to have been destroyed in order to conceal a conspiracy of masculine social superiority, and the version handed down to us fosters discrimination against women. In his discussion of Grass, Mews agrees with the opinion of Ziolowski, who observes that great artists and thinkers are in some measure "mythopoets" (Mews 1983). Grass may therefore be among those articulating the emergence of a new myth of masculinity and femininity.

THE DEVELOPMENT OF THE STORY

The fisherman fishes regularly in the sea – that is, he constantly gropes or searches in the depths; something in him has a connection to the larger, objective psyche. For long periods, nothing arises to help, but his approach is one of waiting and meditating, allowing rather than insisting. Presumably, he needs to connect with something in his soul that will help him with his marriage, since he lives with his wife in a psychological pigsty.

The action begins when his line is seized. He does not have any control in this situation, but rather the deeply hidden material represented by the flounder initiates the dynamic sequence of the story; there is a pull from the unconscious. However, the flounder warns the fisherman that he "should not be good to eat." It is as if the Self knows that it cannot be assimilated by the fisherman at his present level of development and so warns him that it would be best to let it go down again. The flounder's poignant "let me live" is reminiscent of Jung's idea that the Self wants to live its experiment in life and here requests help of the conscious personality so that this may happen. Since the fish disappears back into the depths, we are also reminded of the dictum that the unconscious both wants to become conscious but also does not wish this (Jung 1952, par. 745).

The fisherman seems content to ignore the encounter. We wonder at his apparent lack of any concern for redeeming or healing the flounder's enchantment. The Self speaks, but he is content to let the experience slip away. Indeed, it seems to be because of the flounder's speech that the fisherman may be afraid of it. Here we sense an allusion to the ambivalent nature of the fish, which Jung also indicates may represent lechery, our "untameable properties," which defile the body (1954c, par. 187; 1950, pars. 199, 211). The fish is associated with *concupiscentia* because of its relationship to the mother and love goddess Ishtar, Astarte, or Aphrodite (Jung 1954c, par. 174), so that in the Middle Ages, fish were an allegory of the damned (ibid., par. 187). For one medieval author, the fish may symbolize the tongue, speech, and powers of expression of man, especially when these are sinful (Jung 1950, par. 210). In particular, he warns that the tongue sets on fire "the wheel of birth," which Jung understands as the soul depicted as the wheel of the horoscope – thus the tongue is the destructive, diabolical element within the psyche that can lead to a "catastrophic revolt of all the original components of the psyche" (ibid., par. 212). It is as if the fisherman senses some intimation of the revolution portended by the appearance of the flounder and wants no part of it. His fishing has brought up more than he bargained for. Further pre-Christian amplification of fish symbolism may also cast light on the fisherman's eagerness to dispose of the fish. According to Walker, the early Christian use of fish symbolism was taken over from earlier symbols of the yonic goddess, with an attempt to deny its female-genital significance (1983, p. 314). The fish symbol was a *vesica piscis*, a worldwide symbol of the Great Mother. Fish and womb were synonymous in Greek: *delphos* meant both. Even Jesus, as Jung also indicates, was the son of the Fish-Mother. Thus, the prince, although he sounds masculine, is also loaded with archetypal mother significance for the fisherman.

Not only does the fisherman not display any curiosity, or even attempt to relate to the fish, he also seems to want nothing, as if it does not occur to him that he might be in any way entitled to live more comfortably. The flounder behaves like the serpent in the Garden of Eden – the factor that originates the birth of a new level of consciousness, a split-off, unintegrated part of the Self. But the fisherman ignores this new potential. His wife, however, insists on his returning to the flounder to exploit its energy. It is via the feminine that he is now forced to connect to the power within his own depths – she humiliates him, but she also pushes him into contact with the Self. She must sense some deep resources within him that he cannot utilize. Perhaps she nags him not only out of her own lack of fulfillment in the marriage but also because of her frustration with his passivity. They use each other as selfobjects, to make up for unconscious deficits, and since they are thus narcissistically merged, cannot love the other as a separate individual, but only insofar as each meets the other's needs.

Unwillingly, he returns to the sea, which was previously clear, but is now green and yellow and not so smooth. Psychologically, envy and fear are being stirred up. His call to the flounder reflects his ambivalence, essentially saying, "Come to me, because my wife wants something I'd rather she did not want." From his repressed grandiosity, the squashed energy of the Self, he has to cull enhancement for his demanding, grandiose anima. This process transforms where they live – his intrapsychic structuralization has improved its quality, thanks to his anima inflation.

The fisherman feels better initially, but the inflation feeds on its own greedy needs. The new equilibrium is "too small." Again, the fisherman tries unsuccessfully to resist the pressure from his wife, but she is too powerful, too unloving and unempathic to sense his distress. He returns to the flounder, and now the sea is purple and blue, grey and thick – indicating a heavy, sad, and perhaps bruised state of mind. Again, the inflation works to build a new defensive structure. They now live in the luxury of a "great stone palace."

His wife cannot be satisfied. She pokes at him and says, "Couldn't we be the King. . . . We will be the King." The term "we" indicates that this is a wife who does not feel like an individual, but rather is fused in a psychological merger with her husband. When the fisherman disavows his grandiosity by protesting, "I do not want to be King," she autonomously insists, "I must be King." The symptom often offers a symbolic clue to the deficit; her wish to be a ruler and her lack of differentiation from her husband suggest that she feels powerless and weak and is urgently trying to shore herself up. She does not insist on being queen, presumably because she has no sense of authentic feminine authority. She married a weak man, unable to contact his own power, whose passivity corresponds to her own inner sense of powerlessness. She senses in him the buried key to her own needs, which she cannot otherwise meet.

At this point, the sea, representing the emotional life of the fisherman, is not only dark grey and turbulent but also smells putrid. Something is rotten; decay has begun, the *putrefactio* foretelling the eventual decomposition of the structures that have been built. She is king, but it smells bad. The inflation continues; the anima becomes king of the psyche, but she is described as "quite anxious," and time passes heavily. The success of each new expansion now lasts very little time and does not assuage the pervasive, empty restlessness. The grandiose expansion seems rather to heighten an inner sense of enfeeblement, leading to even more urgent attempts to compensate. She now insists on being emperor.

When the fisherman protests, she openly expresses her devaluation of him: "You are nothing but my husband." He perceives her "shamelessness" and is afraid the flounder will be depleted. In fact, he is ashamed – full of forbidden exhibitionism, now totally split off or disavowed from his consciousness, carried by the image of the wife. The sea is now black, thick and boiling, with a high wind, and he is afraid. But still the flounder gratifies his wife. An extraordinary inflation ensues—she sits on a two-mile-high throne, wearing a three-yard crown. A note of the absurd has entered the story, as if the psyche mocks itself in a parody of excess. The inflation seems to reach psychotic proportions.

The wife now wishes to claim both secular and nonsecular power by also demanding to be pope. In spite of his protests and terror, the fisherman goes back to the flounder, amidst a scene of tremendous turmoil. Yet, in spite of all the uproar, a small patch of blue sky can still be seen, perhaps indicating a window to heaven which is still open, or the possibility of help from above. In despair and hopelessness, he asks and is granted his request. On his return, his wife has become a caricature of ecclesiastical and earthly splendor. Her throne is even higher, she has multiple crowns, and the fisherman seems to be looking at the sun. But she is stiff and lifeless. This is a joyless, life-denying state to be in. Greed consumes her and keeps her awake. She is more empty than ever. The next morning, she demands the power to make the sun and moon rise—"I wish to be like unto God." When the fisherman protests, she flies into a narcissistic rage, revealing how much she is on the edge of fragmentation. She needs total control to defend against her utter helplessness. She wishes to identify with the Self in order to cope with her own lack of personal identity, but she can only connect with the Self via her husband, just as he needs her for the same purpose because both lack relationship to their inner contrasexual bridges to the Self. Likewise, he behaves "like a madman." Complete intrapsychic chaos is now depicted by the image of a great storm, with houses and trees blown away, total darkness, and gigantic tidal waves.

The fisherman conveys her demand to be "like unto God," whereupon the flounder restores them to their original state of living in the pigsty. This ending is open to a variety of interpretations. Psychodynamically, it depicts the completion of a typical cycle of inflation, grandiosity, and despair, especially when the narcissistic character disorder eventually realizes the illusory nature of its grandiosity. Equanimity cannot be attained by the pursuit of grandiose fantasy, because this feeds upon itself. Inflation never truly nourishes or restores the individual's vulnerable real self and risks an inauthentic arrogation of the energy of the Self, while the individual fails to properly separate from immersion in the unconscious. A true relationship between the transpersonal and the personal can thus never be attained (Schwartz-

Salant 1982). However, it is important to note that under certain favorable circumstances, the suffering produced by such a cycle may result in major psychological and spiritual growth. Narcissistic structures may become transformed by the experience of despair, if the Self is able to manifest while the individual's usual defenses against such experience are in abeyance. The suffering necessary for this process may be mediated or instigated by the animus or anima, as seen in this fairy tale.

Therefore, we believe that the return to the pigsty in fact fulfills the wife's request to be "like unto God," in the sense that God can be found (or is born) in the lowest and most humble of settings. The numinosum is found in the archetypal dimension of the complex which possesses us; spiritual development therefore requires wrestling with the complex. After enlightenment, or the attainment of consciousness of the Self, the wife would not identify with its power. Following contact with the archetypal realm, outwardly life seems to go on as before, but consciousness is transformed.

REFERENCES

Bharati, A. 1975. *The Tantric Tradition*. New York: Samuel Weiser, Inc.

Corbett, L. 1987. Transformation of the image of God leading to self initiation into old age. In *Betwixt and Between: Patterns of Masculine and Feminine Initiation*. L. Mahdi, ed. LaSalle, Ill.: Open Court.

Giovacchini, P. 1978. The psychoanalytic treatment of alienated patients. In *New Perspectives on Psychotherapy of the Borderline Adult*. J. Masterson, ed. New York: Brunner-Mazel.

Grass, G. 1978. *The Flounder*. New York: Ballantine Books.

Grunberger, B. 1971. *Narcissism*. New York: International Universities Press.

Hillman, J. 1973. Anima. *Spring*, pp. 97–132.

Jung, C. G. 1927. Woman in Europe. *CW* 10:113–133. Princeton, N.J.: Princeton University Press, 1964.

______. 1928. The relations between the ego and the unconscious. *CW* 7:123–304. Princeton, N.J.: Princeton University Press, 1953.

______. 1944. *Psychology and Alchemy*. *CW*, vol. 12. Princeton, N.J.: Princeton University Press, 1953.

______. 1950. Concerning rebirth. *CW* 9i:113–149. Princeton, N.J.: Princeton University Press, 1959.

______. 1951a. *Aion*. *CW*, vol. 9ii. Princeton, N.J.: Princeton University Press, 1959.

______. 1951b. The psychology of the child archetype. *CW* 9i:151–181. Princeton, N.J.: Princeton University Press, 1959.

———. 1952. Answer to Job. *CW* 11:355–472. Princeton, N.J.: Princeton University Press, 1958.

———. 1954a. Archetypes of the collective unconscious. *CW* 9i:3–41. Princeton, N.J.: Princeton University Press, 1959.

———. 1954b. Concerning the archetypes, with special reference to the anima concept. *CW* 9i:54–73. Princeton, N.J.: Princeton University Press, 1959.

———. 1954c. Psychological aspects of the mother archetype. *CW* 9i:75–111. Princeton, N.J.: Princeton University Press, 1959.

———. 1955–1956. *Mysterium Coniunctionis. CW*, vol. 14. Princeton, N.J.: Princeton University Press, 1963.

Jung, E., and von Franz, M.-L. 1980. *The Grail Legend.* Baltimore: Sigo Press.

Kernberg, O. 1975. *Borderline Conditions and Pathological Narcissism.* New York: Jason Aronson.

Kohut, H. 1971. *The Analysis of the Self.* New York: International Universities Press.

Mews, S. 1983. The Fisherman and His Wife. Gunther Grass's *The Flounder.* In *Critical Perspectives.* New York: AMS Press.

Schwartz-Salant, N. 1982. *Narcissism and Character Transformation.* Toronto: Inner City Books.

Volkan, V. D. 1973. Transitional fantasies in the analysis of a narcissistic personality. *Journal of the American Psychoanalytical Association* 21:351–376.

Walker, B. G. 1983. *The Woman's Encyclopedia of Myths and Secrets.* New York: Harper and Row.

Whitmont, E. C. 1982. *Return of the Goddess.* New York: Crossroad.

Winnicott, D. W. 1975. Aggression in relation to emotional development. In *Through Paediatrics to Psycho-Analysis.* New York: Basic Books.

"Fitcher's Bird" Illustrations of the Negative Animus and Shadow in Persons with Narcissistic Disturbances

Kathrin Asper

Translated by Elizabeth Burr

In Jungian psychology the masculine component in the psyche of a woman is defined as the animus. Its counterpart is the anima, the image of woman in the man. As a rule, psychological jargon has little that is good to say about the animus; indeed the expression has actually become a term of abuse with reference to women.

If C. G. Jung laid the foundations of this genial concept (1921, 1928, 1954, 1951), then the credit goes to Emma Jung for depicting the animus in a more differentiated manner than Jung had originally done. For her the essence of the animus lay in the expressions "will," "deed," "word," and "meaning" (1957, p. 3). Contrasting it with the anima, which Jung, borrowing from H. R. Haggard's *She*, called "she that must be obeyed" (1928, par. 298), Emma Jung cautioned women against regarding their animus unquestioningly as "he that must be obeyed" (1957, pp. 32ff). For too long women had accustomed themselves to obeying men and had internalized this hierarchical order in themselves also. On the contrary, Emma Jung maintained, it is a matter of each woman learning to stand her ground vis-à-vis the animus and to enhance her own femininity, a femininity subject for centuries to undervaluation in the patriarchy.

In this article I would like to speak about the problem of the negatively constellated animus in the psyche of the woman and to connect that theme with fairy-tale images, especially those from the Grimm tale entitled "Fitcher's Bird" (1972, p. 216). In the course of the paper I shall occasionally indicate the resemblance of the negative animus problem to the problem of the man's negative shadow.

SYMPTOMATOLOGY

The symptoms of a negative animus are:

~ rationality,
~ collective judgments,
~ self-destructiveness,
~ destructiveness of others.

In the affected woman it causes:

~ latent depression,
~ defense mechanisms,
~ despair and a sense of powerlessness.

The animus is never at a loss for *rational*-intellectual arguments. These are often just slightly "off," but sound quite considered and are therefore hard to see through.

In my view, such judgments and opinions are not tied to affectivity and do not take the feelings of the woman in question seriously. In other words, she cannot take herself seriously in her feelings; this state of affairs can become so extreme that she does not even feel them anymore. Thus the rationality of the animus is always accompanied with an emotional insecurity and, in severe cases, with a deficiency of feeling. The latter, of course, has little to do with the typological functions that Jung demonstrated. It is not a matter of inferior feeling or of its obverse, highly developed thinking, as the primary function. On the contrary, with the animus problem, thinking is undifferentiated and cannot be equated with the thinking of a primary function. Feeling itself is not at all weak and underdeveloped. The animus-controlled woman is usually quite able to differentiate her feelings and to feel with others.

Yet she often "may" not do so precisely because of her animus-constellation and animus-dominance. The feelings that are repressed and sabotaged are frequently those of autonomy and self-defense, and are thus tied to positive-aggressive tendencies.

Lucy, a woman of forty-five, who suffered intensely from a negative animus, often attacked herself verbally, which she was unconscious of doing; moreover her husband did the same thing, at least according to her interpretation. Internally and externally—on both the subjective and the objective levels—therefore, a masculine power was at work that prevented her from defending herself and presenting things from her point of view. In such situations, she felt decidedly helpless and inwardly empty. It seemed to her as if she had lost her orientation. From a rational standpoint, the arguments advanced either by her or by her husband appeared to be entirely acceptable; from the standpoint of feeling, however, they were not at all. Furthermore, apart from the fact that she did not dare to say this, Lucy had great difficulty in general in becoming aware of her feelings and taking them seriously. During a day when she had once again been in a situation where she could not assert herself, she had the following dream:

> *All my teeth have fallen out, and with horror and despair, I see my toothless mouth in the mirror.*

This image stayed with her for a long time and was a warning to her. She felt toothless in the face of the animus assertions that were working on her, and she could not reply because, figuratively speaking, she lacked the teeth to chew and grind the animus judgments, i.e., to analyze and contest them.

Also associated with rational animus judgments are *collective* "dos and don'ts." These are just as sabotaging of one's own standpoint as rational opinions. Nor are they likely to enable the woman to formulate her feeling values and, on the basis of these, to assume her own standpoint. In our patriarchally imprinted society, collective values always have a patriarchal bias and, since they are supported and shared by the collective, are very hard to see through.

There is an episode in the well-known Cinderella tale from the Grimm collection (1972, p. 121) that represents this phenomenon perfectly. You remember that Cinderella, who does all the humble kitchen chores in mute submission, is nonetheless tormented by the stepmother and the two nasty stepsisters. Her misery experiences a positive turning point, though, at the moment when the father is about to go to a fair and asks his daughters what he should bring home for them. The vain sisters wish for "pearls," "jewels," and "beautiful dresses." Last of all Cinderella asks her father merely for the green "branch" that knocks against his "hat." In a figurative sense the wish is "to get onto a green branch" in the German idiom, a longing for one's own inner development. In the tale there actually is such a branch; it even knocks the hat off the father's head. Hats, especially men's hats, are symbols of collective values, which a man represents according to his profession. One thinks of the bishop's mitre, the hunter's cap, the doctor's hat, and the cook's toque, for example. Now, if such a hat falls off, the collective values behind which Cinderella can hide likewise tumble to the ground. And instead of "old hats," the possibility of assuming one's own standpoint autonomously has been opened up, a standpoint that lies beyond the realm of dos and don'ts.

As is already evident from what has been said so far, the animus is *self-destructive*. It turns against one's own person, and its most familiar refrain is surely this: "I am not worth anything; I can't do anything; nobody likes me; I am stupid and ugly, and I have no right to exist." These are very deep-seated convictions, which in the first instance cannot be grasped as clearly and obviously as described here. Only when consciousness about the problem has made some headway do they appear so precisely and comprehensibly in verbal form.

The animus is not only self-destructive; it is also *destructive of the other*. Just as explosively demeaning as in its self-destructive aspect, the animus is equally capable of turning outward and of reducing and ruining other people, things, and situations. However, we must see and understand this feature in the sense of psychic release, too. If it affects others in this destructive way, the subject has thereby rid herself temporarily of self-destructiveness. Here one can speak of a projective identification (Gordon 1965): a part of one's own ego-identity is split off and located in the outer world. Projective identification is always more than ordinary projection. In ordinary projection, an unconscious component is displaced onto the outer environment; in projective identification, a part of the ego–self identity is split off and located in another person.

In this connection we can again draw on Cinderella and her stepsisters for illustration. Cinderella is obviously self-destructive, while her stepsisters are destructive of the other, that is, they deal destructively with Cinderella. If we picture Cinderella and her stepsisters as parts of a single psyche, we can speak definitely of two systems which alternate in having the upper hand. One system is destructive of the other; hence it attacks other people and is symbolized by the stepsisters. The other system is self-destructive and is represented by Cinderella. There are many people today who suffer from a negative animus problem. They are often very condemnatory in their relations with other people, but they can also very frequently direct the destructiveness inward and attack themselves.

Let us now move on from the symptoms of a negative animus problem to consider its effects on the woman herself. The problem under discussion produces a *chronically latent depression.* In other words, the psychic background of such a woman is tinged with darkness.

On the one hand, this latent depression can be *warded off*, for example, by "manic defense," in the sense that everything is laughingly skimmed over and there are simply no problems because none are allowed. On the other hand, destructiveness of the other may come into force, in which case the outer world is destructively depreciated. In this way, the subject can get rid of negative components and enhance herself. This, too, is a defensive form of latent depression.

The negative animus also plunges the woman it affects into *despair*: when the self-destructive impulses are at work, the despair that arises gives her a feeling of impotence (Lucy's tooth dream) and at the same time the sensation of not being coherent but rather "in pieces." This is called fragmentation. Internally the woman's animus chops and tears her self to pieces, a tendency that will be mentioned at greater length in relation to the tale "Fitcher's Bird." The fragmentation is felt as extremely unpleasant, and she tries each time to return to a state of coherence as quickly as possible. Her fragmentation and the reaction evoked by it confer on the woman dominated by the animus the quality of drivenness that has been so frequently cited and described, although not interpreted in this light.

CAUSES OF THE NEGATIVE ANIMUS PROBLEM

What are the causes of such a pronounced animus problem? I think it is misleading to speak of an animus without reference to its aetiology. Rather, I hold that a negative animus of this type is very often a symptom of a deep personality disturbance. I see the negative animus problem described above as tied to a negative mother problem. To express this more specifically, the negative animus is a symptom of the so-called *narcissistic disturbance* (Asper 1987). On the archetypal level, the negative Great Mother lies behind such a disturbance, with the result that the affected person cannot love him- or herself adequately, suffers from a pronounced self-esteem problem and is consequently disturbed in his or her sense of identity and autonomy. Taking the perspective of developmental psychology, one could say that such a disturbance is rooted in an unsuccessful mother–child relationship. As we know today, if the "fit" between mother and child is not optimal, grave disturbances are engendered, one of which is the narcissistic disorder. The reasons for this may lie with the personal mother, in many instances an unloved child herself, who can neither love her child adequately nor care for it tenderly. It would be wrong, though, to declare the mother entirely responsible. Ultimately there are many reasons for an unsuccessful life beginning, among them the early death of the mother, partial deprivations (separations from the mother determined, for example, by illness), war, and marital or material crises. Another contributing factor to such a disorder, it should not be forgotten, may be the incapacity of the child (e.g., because of sickness) to constellate maternal feelings in the mother. For one does not just *have* a mother; one also *creates* her for oneself (the same is true regarding the father). An emotionally abandoned child of this type not only suffers from a lack of maternal and solicitous attitudes, but also is not really seen, or "mirrored," as the technical term puts it (Asper 1987, Kohut 1971, Winnicott 1977). Only the child who has been optimally mirrored and whose self-esteem has been "brought forth by love" is in a position to develop a strong ego and a correspondingly positive sense of identity. The child who has not been mirrored enough has little or no confidence in herself and no secure inner foundation, nor is she able later in life to affirm herself adequately. Concomitant with this is a certain self-alienation in the sense that the self as one's true nature cannot emerge clearly.

Nevertheless, in order to survive, the child develops survival strategies. One of these is adaptation and the endeavor to serve the family ideology with the aim of at least being able to "buy" love through worthy conduct. This strategy entails an emotional division of feelings into "good" ones and "bad" ones. The bad feelings such as fear, rage, hatred, envy, grief, and helplessness are repressed, and only the good feelings are shown to the surrounding world. Therefore, in Jungian psychology we speak of the true personality, which is not shown, and the persona, which appears outwardly and shields the true personality (Jung 1928). For these entities Winnicott coined the now widely used designations "true self" and "false self" (Winnicott 1971). Recalling the tale of Cinderella again, we can designate the stepsisters as the persona or false self, while finding in the mute Cinderella the true personality or true self.

Another survival strategy is the animus, which claims our special attention in this paper. According to Erich Neumann (1973), the patriarchal element is originally conveyed to the infant not so much by the father but already much earlier by the animus aspects of the mother. An example of this would be a situation in which the baby has had to adjust to a strict feeding schedule and when it senses its real needs – in this case hunger – must cry for hours without being heard or noticed. A child who undergoes many such instances of her needs being rigidly neglected day after day, with time becomes silent. Her needs are not heeded, nor is her rage observed. Subsequently she no longer expresses either. From this experience the latent depression that was mentioned earlier develops. The rigidity of the mother (and perhaps that of other attachment figures) is gradually internalized and molded into a firm constituent of the personality, which we call the animus. The animus then becomes a vehicle by which the child attempts to master existence in the manner described above: through rationality, overlooking one's own feelings, and adapting to collective values. The impulses destructive of self and others that have already been discussed are also linked to this strategy. The negative animus thus signifies a premature constellation of the archetypal masculine in the psyche of the woman. From the more personalistic perspective of developmental psychology, it replicates the rigid animus of the attachment figure from early childhood. As a symptom of narcissistic disturbance, it is associated with a pronounced self-esteem problem.

THE NARCISSISTIC PROBLEM AND THE MASCULINE PSYCHE

I believe that men, too, can gain an understanding of the narcissistic problem as described here, since as we all know it is encountered not only in women but also in men.

For this reason, I would pose the logical question whether one must then assume, for example, a negative animus problem in men as well as women. Men, of course, can present the symptoms of a negative animus listed earlier, namely rationality, adaptation to collective values, self-destructiveness, and destructiveness of others.

Therefore we might say that men, too, can exhibit a negative animus. But this statement brings us into conflict with the classical Jungian concepts according to which the animus is valid for the psyche of the woman and the anima for the psyche of the man. We can begin to solve this problem by noting that what appears in the woman as the negative animus is a negative shadow in the man. In this sense, the negative animus corresponds to the man's shadow. The leading negative aspect of the masculine shadow in our society is rape. The negative animus in fact rapes the woman's femininity and her feelings. In the man, it is the rapist's shadow that fails to take his anima or anima feelings seriously and gives them no chance to be heard.[1]

Yet it seems to me that the whole issue creates fewer problems for the man than for the woman because we live in a patriarchal era, in which patriarchal values are collectively approved values. So the man can identify with them better than the woman can. His identity is less disturbed by this than is that of the woman, who should be able to identify with collective feminine values. The absence of such values, as well as the impact of schooling and upbringing, causes the woman to identify with masculine collective values. If a narcissistic disturbance exists in the background of her psyche, then, having already received a masculine imprint too early and too emphatically, her psyche is

---

[1]Another way of explaining the problem in the masculine psyche could be based on the idea proposed by others, i.e., Hillman (1985) and Kast (1984). They suggest that the anima and the animus exist in both women and men. As compelling as this idea may be, I have in my experience not seen enough analysands where this is the case. Additionally the delimiting of shadow and anima in women and shadow and animus in men raises problems which are beyond the scope of this paper.

further reinforced by masculine values, and she finds herself inevitably and imperceptibly in a state of marked self-alienation. Her feminine self is thus overshadowed by the patriarchal superstructure of her personality and so is hindered in its manifestation. This does not happen to the man to the same extent, because the collective values with which he identifies constitute part of his masculine self. His self-alienation is accordingly less evident than that of the woman. But like the woman he, too, becomes estranged from his feelings and suppresses, or rapes, his anima. Thus he must liberate his anima from the embrace of his negative shadow. In this sense, his anima becomes the psychic component which Jung could say was "she that must be obeyed."

Now I would like to examine the tale "Fitcher's Bird" (Grimm 1972, pp. 216–220), retold here in brief, with regard to the negative animus problem in the woman and concurrently—insofar as possible—to illuminate the man's negative shadow problem.

Fitcher's Bird

There was once a wizard, who, in the disguise of a poor beggar with a basket on his back, was known to lure pretty girls from their homes, carrying them whence no one knew.

One day he came to the home of a man with three pretty daughters. The eldest, while handing him some bread, was forced to jump into his basket, with but a touch from the beggar himself. Thereupon he hurriedly took her away to his magnificent house in a dark forest, where she was given all she desired.

In time, he set forth on a journey, having first given her the keys to the house with the condition that she not enter one room "on pain of death." Likewise he had entrusted her with an egg which she must carefully preserve lest misfortune occur. Overcome by her curiosity, she entered the forbidden room and in her fright, dropped the egg in the great bloody vat containing butchered human remains in the middle of the room. Alas, the bloodstained egg served as evidence of her deed. Upon the wizard's return, she had to atone with her life.

The wizard fetched the second daughter who succumbed to the same fate.

The clever and wily third sister, brought to the wizard's house in like fashion, when faced with the keys and the egg, took great care to first secure the egg and then entered the forbidden room where she beheld the ghastly scene of her butchered sisters. She reassembled their body parts and once intact, the maidens returned to life with great rejoicing. Upon his return, the wizard observed the blood-free egg and said, "You have stood the test, you shall be my bride."

Having lost his power over her and now forced to do her bidding, he had to carry, without rest, a basketful of gold on his back to her parents, while she prepared for the wedding. She said, "I shall look through my little window and watch to see if you stop on the way." Unbeknownst to the wizard, the clever bride had hidden her sisters in the basket with the instructions to send help from home. Whenever he stood to rest, a voice from the basket cried out, "I am looking through my little window. Go on at once."

Meanwhile the bride, having sent wedding invitations to the wizard's friends, placed an ornamented and wreathed grinning skull in the garret window. She then plunged herself into a barrel of honey and rolled herself in feathers from her featherbed, and, disguised as a wondrous bird, she set out to meet the wedding guests, who asked,

> "O, Fitcher's bird, how com'st thou here?"
> "I come from Fitcher's house quite near."
> "And what may the young bride be doing?"
> "From cellar to garret she's swept all clean,
> And now from the window she's peeping, I we'en."

At last she met the returning bridegroom, who asked the same, and, spying that decorated skull which he thought to be his bride, he nodded and greeted it kindly. When he and his guests had entered the house, the brothers and kinsmen of the bride arrived in time to bolt all the doors, set fire to the house, and the wizard and his cronies had to burn.

The tale "Fitcher's Bird" belongs to the category of so-called Bluebeard or maiden-murderer tales (Aarne and Thompson 1961, p. 311). The most famous version is that of Perrault (ibid., p. 312) entitled "Bluebeard," which is also related to the well-known Grimm tale exemplifying the "robber-bridegroom" type (Grimm 1972, p. 200–204; Aarne and Thompson 1961, p. 955).

The leitmotif of our tale—and it is one of the cruelest in the entire world of fairy tales—is the chopping and cutting up of the feminine. Twice the wizard succeeds in dismembering a woman:

the sisters of the tale's heroine. The latter, however, the third sister, he cannot cut to pieces; with her cunning and ego-strength, she is able to convict the evildoer, who is then captured and burned by her brothers and kinsmen.

In the following interpretation, I regard the wizard as a symbol for the negative animus of a woman. An animus of this kind is always cutting and chopping. It leaves no part of one's intrinsic nature or sense of identity unscathed, so that a woman affected by it often experiences herself as fragmented. In the tale, the animus-wizard appears as self-destructive if we assume that all the figures occurring in a tale are parts, or aspects, of a single personality.

Yet how easily women attach themselves to him! Scarcely has he touched one than she springs, as if drawn by magic, into his "basket," and he can carry her off as booty. This is exactly what happens in reality with the negative animus problem. On the subjective level, such women believe their animus implicitly and fall blindly into its trap by not questioning its judgments. They express their own negative judgments about themselves quite naturally and credit these judgments. On the objective level, they believe a man and cling to him even if they have to suffer severely under him.

In this connection, I shall return to Lucy and her story. Lucy was the third of four children from what would be described on the basis of external observation as a good, middle-class family. She had two older brothers and one younger sister. Her father was an official: a stern, authoritarian man who organized his day and his activities with meticulous precision. Honoring such values as accuracy, absolute honesty, objectivity, clarity, and conscientiousness, he saw to it that his children also adhered to these values. Clearly a man of patriarchal stamp, he considered the hierarchical order in his family to be God-given and therefore sacrosanct and thoroughly natural. His wife, Lucy's mother, was a quiet, sensitive woman. Partly for this reason, she submitted to her husband in everything and trusted his opinions and conceptions, even when they went against her own feelings. She thus obliterated herself in her own nature with undue vehemence, leading a shadowy existence in the shadow of the husband she dreaded. The fact that she never developed into a strong and autonomous personality was partly related to her having once been an emotionally abandoned child who never received adequate loving attention from her parents. Moreover, the social status of her family of origin was inferior to that of her husband. One can infer, then, that Lucy's mother was already a narcissistically disturbed woman long before she tragically and unconsciously inflicted a narcissistic injury on Lucy (and perhaps the other children, too). Again and again, research on narcissism indicates that the mothers of narcissistically wounded persons were themselves already narcissistically disturbed.

Lucy experienced her mother as unempathic, rigid, and emotionally abandoning of her. By siding with Lucy's father whenever there was an argument, she hurt Lucy's feelings, even though this was not her intention at all. So it was no wonder that Lucy could develop no confidence in herself and was particularly ill-prepared to trust her perceptions, observations, and feelings. Since her father and, following his lead, her mother, too, classified feelings as sentimental, Lucy fell into a peculiar internal and external vacuum, which eventually led her to rely more on collective values and rational arguments than on her own feelings and intentions. In addition, she could secure her parents' love only through achievement and good behavior; this resulted in a strongly marked persona (false self). Her animus found expression in her habit of discounting every personal emotion as worthless and stupid. She was full of self-destructive impulses and, without knowing it, constantly criticized herself. Her sense of self-esteem was practically nil. At the age of twenty, she met a very successful man who possessed all the qualities that she so fervently wished for herself. He was self-assured, strong, and successful. In the language of the fairy tale, Lucy "jumped" literally into his "basket," married him, and began a common life with him.

What happened, though? It became more and more apparent that Lucy was dominated by her husband. Now she had the destructive element in her outer environment as well. He showed her up in front of other people, criticized her, and regarded her as illogical, irrational, and sentimental. He checked on her constantly, threatened to withdraw his love at every opportunity, and did not even shrink from attacking her physically on occasion. He was unpredictable and shifted unexpectedly between unfriendliness and amiability. He made her responsible for his failures. He abused her sexually and constantly devalued her as a woman. None of these characteristics was visible to the outer world, however, and he was reputed to be a charming and successful man.

For a long time, Lucy found it difficult to admit that her husband had these negative traits. She loved him and hated him at the same time, yet without plainly admitting the latter feeling to herself. On account of his constant devaluation of her, she fell more and more into dark, somber moods, which gradually hardened into a depression. It was this that finally brought her into analysis. Here it became evident that behind the competent, pretty, and fully adjusted woman there lay a massive self-esteem problem, with the animus problem and its self-destructive elements occupying the foreground. In the course of a long, analytically oriented therapy, Lucy's strongly self-destructive impulses came to light. Her condition was approached in such a way – and this I can outline only roughly – that her narcissistic wound with its leading symptom of disturbed self-esteem was the focus of attention. In such a case a specific therapeutic procedure is indicated, which is the subject of my book *Verlassenheit und Selbstentfremdung* (Asper 1987). In order to be able to approach the narcissistic wound and support the weak ego, it is first necessary to conduct the analysis reductively, and by way of transference and countertransference to reconstruct the childhood history. Thus the events from that time can be affectively reexperienced and gradually integrated. The broken-off dialogue with the inner child of long ago must be taken up again, and insofar as is possible, the child within the adult should be understood in its traumas and frustrations. The possibility thereby arises of establishing little by little a secure inner foundation, and in the course of time, the empathic analyst may be integrated as a good inner object. If this procedure succeeds, such analysands can develop positive maternal attitudes toward themselves. The whole treatment of the negative animus problem must be seen within the framework of the overall therapy of a narcissistic disturbance. This therapy is aimed at constellating the good inner mother as substratum and guarantor of a better and stronger sense of identity in the psyche. The growth of a sense of identity is paralleled by a reduction of the negative animus, which becomes gentler and more sympathetic. Along with Lucy's internal disturbance, the problem with her husband also had to be addressed, since, through his shadow, he coincided to such an extent with her own negative animus. As she became stronger, she succeeded better in demarcating herself from her husband and in asserting herself beside him. Lucy is still dealing with these problems, and whether a divorce will occur cannot be foreseen.

Now let us return to the fairy tale. In it the wizard manages to entice each of the three sisters, one after the other, into the woods. Not until the third sister is the turning point precipitated. We can interpret the third sister as the third attempt to deal with this chopping animus. In fairy tales, generally, three is a constantly recurring number; it symbolizes the smallest possible number by which to signify a plurality in an abstract way. It also refers to a masculine, dynamic number that progressively induces a new, fourth state. The three sisters thus stand for a number of attempts to overcome the wizard. First the wizard gives each sister in turn an egg with the request that she keep it safely until he returns. He also forbids her to enter a certain room. Here we have the well-known fairy-tale motif of the forbidden room. Although the room may not be entered on pain of death, such a prohibition is always violated in fairy tales and, to be sure, in life as well. The room contains the basin with the chopped-up women's bodies in it. On no account, therefore, does the wizard want anyone to find out his secret; he is careful to see that no one should discover his shadow and perceive it. The same is true in reality. Lucy's husband did everything he could to prevent her from accusing him and calling attention to his shadow. Whenever she dared to point it out to him, he rebuffed her in a grandiose manner and reviled her to such a degree that she no longer saw any chance at all of adhering to her correct perception and so slipped back into self-accusation. Even if the woman is conscious of an inner problem conditioned by the negative animus, it is still extremely difficult for her not to be taken in by the judgments of the animus, which really are infamous and evil. The animus is extraordinarily creative in mounting new attacks on her, so that a certain strength is required simply to prohibit that.

The first two sisters were cut to pieces by the wizard, but the youngest succeeded in depriving him of his power. Let us look more closely at how this happens.

Both of the older sisters dropped the egg into the "bloody basin" and could not wash or scrape off the blood, with the result that the villain chopped them up and dismembered them. What does the egg stand for? From ancient times, the egg has been a universal symbol of the creation that grows out of it. In the context of the individual psyche, the egg represents the self in the sense of one's true nature. The animus problem in these cases shakes one fundamentally, to the core. The first two sisters could not delimit themselves and were contaminated in their innermost selves by the cruelty of the wizard. This is symbolized by the blood, which sticks to the egg. They could not defend themselves and were chopped to pieces. The affected woman experiences such a situation not as depression but as sheer stupefying despair in which she has lost her identity. At such moments, which can last a very long time indeed, she feels that she no longer exists; she fragments and can answer neither the animus within nor the partner who exhibits analogous negative characteristics. In order to regain some awareness of herself in this fragmentation, it often happens that she seeks to recharge herself physically (which corresponds to the small child's displacement of interest onto its own body, for example, by engaging in stereotyped movements, masturbation, and sucking). I have often observed that adults indulge in excessive promiscuity so as to regain body awareness and ego-identity through the sexual act. Or else they inflict physical pain on themselves by striking, scratching, or pinching particular parts of their bodies. Masturbation can sometimes be understood from a similar viewpoint. This involvement with one's own body enables the almost entirely submerged sense of self-esteem to rise again – until the next time – and then the pendulum swings so far back again that the animus and/or its exponent in the outer world can cut the woman to pieces once more, because she is not capable of protecting and defending her egg, i.e., her self.

At last the third sister (the third attempt always represents a developmental step and precipitates a turning point) shows sufficient ego-strength to put the egg aside before she enters the forbidden room. She *is* able to protect her true personality and to uncover the secret of the animus or that of its exponent in the outer world. She sees his shadow and perceives that he actually dismembers the feminine and thus kills it. A fairly long time and a long analysis is usually required before one can fully realize what the animus or a corresponding partner is doing to oneself. Only when the third sister's ego-strength has grown enough does the turning point follow; then she can reassemble her sisters, which is equivalent to seeing what happened to her in the past in a different light and so making it whole again.

This time, when the wizard returns home, he finds to his astonishment that the egg is spotless. He no longer has any power over the third sister. He must do whatever she commands. In other words, autonomy is now with the heroine of the tale. She tells him that she intends to prepare for the wedding and that it is his task to carry a basket full of gold to her parents. Without his knowledge she puts her two sisters into the basket, covers them with gold, and attaches the basket to the wizard's back. Now he must hurry; the moment he stops to rest she will see him and drive him on. As he walks, nearly collapsing under the load, the sisters hidden in the basket order him to continue. Finally he arrives at the house of his bride's parents. Meanwhile she has made arrangements for the wedding celebration and has invited the friends of the villain. Next she takes a skull with grinning teeth, adorns it with jewelry and a garland of flowers, and sets it in the attic window. Then she plunges herself into a barrel full of honey, cuts open her featherbed, and rolls herself in the feathers so that she looks like a strange bird and no one can recognize her. After that she goes out and meets some of the wedding guests, who ask:

> "O, Fitcher's bird, how com'st thou here?"

The dialogue continues:

> "I come from Fitcher's house quite near."
> "And what may the young bride be doing?"
> "From cellar to garret she's swept all clean,
> And now from the window she's peeping, I ween."

At last she meets the bridegroom, who poses the same questions and receives the same answers. He looks up and actually sees the skull, but believes that it is his bride and nods to it. When he is finally inside the house, however, the bride's brothers and kinsmen bolt the doors, so that no one can escape, and set the house on fire. Thus the wizard and his cronies are destroyed by fire.

Let us unravel the symbolism of this part of the tale and try to interpret it on a psychic level. Three points are important:

- the skull,
- the transformation of the bride into a bird by means of honey and feathers,
- the final defeat of the wizard by the brothers and kinsmen.

Instead of confronting the bridegroom herself, the girl sets a skull in the attic window. One way to understand this symbolism can be seen as follows: with the skull, she shows him something that is dead. Having an intense relation to death and killing, he finds the skull alluring. Death is intrinsically the shadow of life, the reverse side of existence. If we take these thoughts further, we might say that she shows him her shadow. This makes psychological sense in that she could not delimit herself from evil for a long time and fell into it again and again. To delimit ourselves from evil, we must mobilize what is called the shadow. As a child, the narcissistically wounded person had to suppress so-called negative impulses such as rage, aggression, and hate in order to adapt to the family ideology. Now it is extremely important that he or she learn to make these impulses conscious so that they can be engaged in a positive way. Women who suffer from the negative animus problem under discussion can hardly distinguish themselves from their animus; believing it implicitly, they are likewise taken in by men with analogous traits and fall into their trap. It is therefore vital to practice self-defense, and for this one needs one's shadow as well as a periodic willingness to be difficult and not always to please others. This may also lead to change in a partner who possesses the negative characteristics described above. Whoever has learned not to listen to sabotaging assertions on every occasion nor to let oneself be cut to pieces by them will sometimes make the astonishing discovery that the animus and/or the partner suddenly turns toward one and becomes a little friendlier.

The heroine of our fairy tale escapes by transforming herself into a strange bird. In their *Anmerkungen zu den Kinder- und Hausmärchen der Brüder Grimm*, Bolte and Polivka observe that tarring and feathering is an old punishment for sexual promiscuity and slander (1963, p. 412). Of course, in our tale honey is applied instead of tar, but honey clearly has the same function as tar, namely to make the feathers stick. Does the heroine of the tale submit herself to a kind of self-punishment for promiscuity and slander? It seems to me that such a motif has psychological relevance in the sense that a woman who lets herself be chopped up by her animus and/or an analogous partner could be said to practice self-abuse and abuse of her femininity, for she lets herself be used in the ugliest manner. And by doing so, she slanders herself, becoming alienated from her true nature. The animus problem always includes self-alienation, because the woman does not listen to herself or take her feelings, impulses, thoughts, and perceptions seriously. It is vital that she become conscious of this, for consciousness will enable her to depotentiate the animus.

The wizard is defeated by the bride's brothers and kinsmen. The narcissistic disturbance and the negative animus problem entailed by it always signify a certain self-alienation (Asper 1987). It is essential that the woman concerned find her way to herself. If she does, then there is a chance that the negative animus will be superseded by the positive animus, which, like the brothers in the tale, is devoted to her very own being. We could also say that it is important to find one's way to endogamous libido (Jung 1952, par. 117, par. 664), i.e., kinship libido (Jung 1946, par. 431), because it is always that libido which constitutes the precondition for finding one's way to one's true self. Endogamous, or kinship, libido is devoted to the subject and so is narcissistic. We need self-love in order to be able to find ourselves. And finally we can say that self-affirmation is that power by which we succeed in depriving the negative animus of its power. With regard to the man, it is essential that he recognize his rapacious and inferior shadow so that he can liberate his feeling side, his anima, from it. Viewed collectively, the patriarchy is a narcissistic insult to the woman, or purely and simply to the feminine, and therefore equally to the man's anima. The woman is wounded in her self by one-sided patriarchal norms, and the man sustains an injury to his feeling side. The negative animus problem and the negative masculine shadow problem are grave enemies of the self that block the path of individuation. Whoever can gain insight into these connections not only is doing something for himself or herself, but also is contributing in a small way to an altered collective consciousness.

REFERENCES

Aarne, A., and Thompson, S. 1961. *The Types of the Folktale*. Helsinki: Academia Scientarium Fennica, 1981.

Asper, K. 1987. *Verlassenheit und Selbstentfremdung*. Olten and Freiburg im Breisgau: Walter Verlag.

Bolte, J., and Polivka, G. 1963. *Anmerkungen zu den Kinder- und Hausmärchen der Brüder Grimm*, vol. 1. Hildesheim: Georg Olms Verlagsbuchhandlung.

Gordon, R. 1965. The concept of projective identification: an evaluation. *Journal of Analytical Psychology* 10/2: 127–149.

Grimm, Brothers. 1972. *The Complete Grimm's Fairy Tales*, M. Hunt, trans. J. Stern, ed. New York: Pantheon Books.

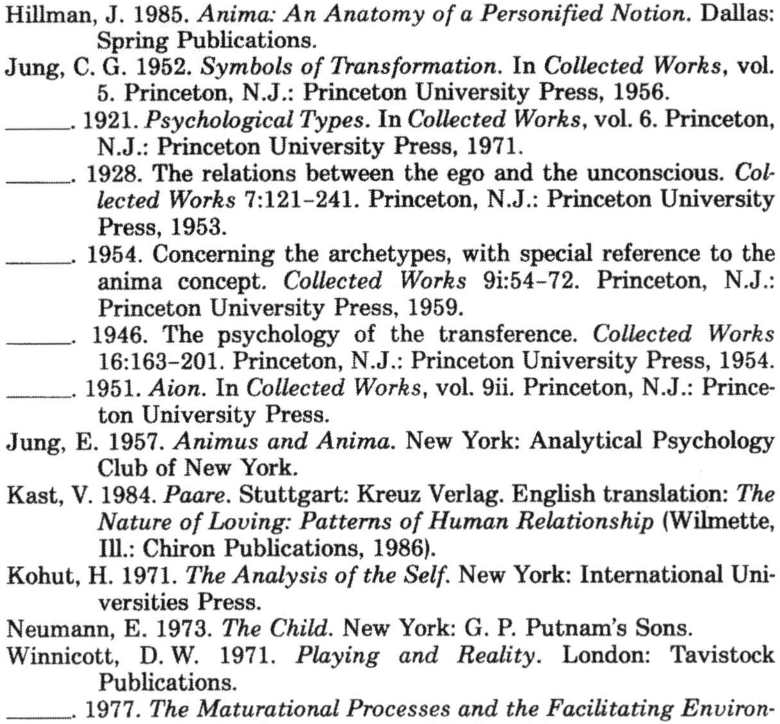

Hillman, J. 1985. *Anima: An Anatomy of a Personified Notion.* Dallas: Spring Publications.

Jung, C. G. 1952. *Symbols of Transformation.* In *Collected Works*, vol. 5. Princeton, N.J.: Princeton University Press, 1956.

______. 1921. *Psychological Types.* In *Collected Works*, vol. 6. Princeton, N.J.: Princeton University Press, 1971.

______. 1928. The relations between the ego and the unconscious. *Collected Works* 7:121–241. Princeton, N.J.: Princeton University Press, 1953.

______. 1954. Concerning the archetypes, with special reference to the anima concept. *Collected Works* 9i:54–72. Princeton, N.J.: Princeton University Press, 1959.

______. 1946. The psychology of the transference. *Collected Works* 16:163–201. Princeton, N.J.: Princeton University Press, 1954.

______. 1951. *Aion.* In *Collected Works*, vol. 9ii. Princeton, N.J.: Princeton University Press.

Jung, E. 1957. *Animus and Anima.* New York: Analytical Psychology Club of New York.

Kast, V. 1984. *Paare.* Stuttgart: Kreuz Verlag. English translation: *The Nature of Loving: Patterns of Human Relationship* (Wilmette, Ill.: Chiron Publications, 1986).

Kohut, H. 1971. *The Analysis of the Self.* New York: International Universities Press.

Neumann, E. 1973. *The Child.* New York: G. P. Putnam's Sons.

Winnicott, D. W. 1971. *Playing and Reality.* London: Tavistock Publications.

______. 1977. *The Maturational Processes and the Facilitating Environment.* New York: International Universities Press.

"The Goose Girl" Puella and Transformation

Ladson Hinton

An old queen, whose husband had been dead for many years, had a very beautiful daughter. When she grew up, she was betrothed to a prince in a distant country. When the marriage date approached, the queen packed clothes and jewels, gold and silver, cups and ornaments, and everything suitable for royalty, all out of love for her daughter.

She sent a waiting-woman to travel with her and to place her hand into that of the bridegroom. Each received a horse, and the princess's horse was named Falada and could speak.

Before the departure, the queen went to her bedroom and cut her finger with a knife, letting three drops of blood fall onto a piece of white linen. She gave this to her daughter, saying, "Dear child, take good care of this; it will stand you in good stead on your journey." There was a sorrowful farewell, and the princess hid the linen next to her breast, mounted her horse, and embarked on her journey.

After a time, she became very thirsty and asked the waiting-woman to fetch some water in her cup from the stream. The waiting-woman responded by telling her to get down herself and drink. She said she did not choose to be the princess's servant.

The girl was so thirsty she just dismounted and drank directly from the stream, because the servant would not fetch her precious cup. As the poor princess drank, she said, "Alas," and the drops of blood answered, "If your mother knew this, it would break her heart."

The royal bride remained humble and said nothing, but got back on her horse once more. They rode a few miles under a scorching sun, and the princess was soon thirsty again. When they reached a river, she called out to her waiting-woman to get her some water in the golden cup, completely forgetting all that had gone before.

Now the waiting-woman was more haughty than ever and told her, "If you want to drink, get the water for yourself. I won't be your servant."

The princess was so thirsty she again dismounted and knelt by the water, saying, "Ah me!" and the drops of blood answered again, "If your mother knew this, it would break her heart."

While she was drinking, the piece of linen with the three drops of blood fell out of her blouse and floated away, but the princess was so fearful she didn't notice. The waiting-woman did see and was very happy because she knew the princess had now become weak and powerless. When they went to remount, the waiting-woman demanded the horse Falada for herself, giving the girl her own nag in exchange.

The princess not only gave way in the exchange of horses, but was also ordered to give up her royal robes and put on the servant's garments. Then, under threat of death, she had to swear an oath that she would tell no creature at the court what had taken place. Falada observed these happenings. After the exchange, they set off again.

There was great rejoicing when they arrived at the castle. The prince, her betrothed, thought the waiting-woman was his bride and lifted her from her horse and took her up into the castle. However, the old king looked out and saw the delicate, pretty girl standing below in the courtyard and asked the false bride about her companion. The woman told him she had brought her for company and that the girl should be put to work.

After reflection, the king suggested she work with a little boy named Conrad, tending the geese. This was done. Soon after, the false bride asked the king to have Falada's head cut off, saying the horse had annoyed her. Actually, she feared the horse would speak and tell the truth of things.

When the princess heard about that, she offered the man employed in the task a piece of gold for a service: to nail up Falada's head in the great dark gateway to the town, through which she passed morning and evening.

This was done, and in the morning when she passed through the gateway with Conrad, she spoke to the head, "Alas! dear Falada, there thou hangest." And the head answered, "Alas! Queen's daughter, there thou gangest. If thy mother knew thy fate, her heart would break with grief so great."

She and Conrad went on out of the town, into the fields with the geese. In the meadow, the princess sat down on the grass and let down her hair. It shone like gold, and little Conrad was so delighted, he tried to pluck some out. But she said:

"Blow, blow little breeze,
And Conrad's hat seize.
Let him join in the chase
While away it is whirled,
Till my tresses are curled
And I rest in my place."

A strong wind came up, blowing his hat away, and he had to run after it. By the time he returned, she had finished putting up her hair and he couldn't get a single strand. Conrad became very sulky at this and would not speak. Finally, they went home in the evening.

The next day, the exact same events transpired with Falada's head, with the princess's hair, and with the wind blowing away Conrad's hat. He went to the king and told him he was so vexed by the maiden that he didn't want to tend the geese with her anymore. The king asked why, and Conrad described in detail all that had happened.

The old king ordered Conrad to continue as usual, and he hid himself behind the dark gateway so he could hear the princess speaking to Falada's head. Then he hid behind a bush in the field, and heard and saw all that happened there. He went back to the castle.

Upon the goose girl's return in the evening, the king called her aside and questioned her. However, she said she could not tell him or any creature, having sworn under threat of death. He pressed her strongly, but she would not give in to his entreaties. Finally, he told her that if she wouldn't tell him, perhaps she could tell the stove. He went outside and stood by the pipes from the stove, so he could hear. Alone, the girl tearfully told her whole story to the stove.

The king came back and told her to come away from the stove then and had her dressed in royal robes. She looked extremely beautiful. The old king told his son about the situation, that he had a false bride who was a waiting-woman, but that the true bride was indeed this so-called goose girl.

The young prince was totally charmed. They held a great banquet to which all the court was invited. The bridegroom sat at the head of the table, with the princess on one side and the waiting-woman on the other. The woman was so dazzled, she didn't recognize the princess in her brilliant apparel.

When everyone had eaten and drunk and were merry, the old king put a riddle to the waiting-woman. He asked her, "What does a person deserve who deceives his master?" and told the whole story. He ended by asking, "What doom does he deserve?"

The false bride answered, "No better than this. He must be put stark naked into a barrel stuck with nails, and be dragged along by two white horses from street to street till he is dead."

"That is your own doom," said the king, "and the judgment shall be carried out."

When the sentence was fulfilled, the young prince married his true bride, and they ruled their kingdom together in peace and happiness.

"The Goose Girl," a beautiful, moving story, is a classic tale of feminine development. In the beginning, there is symbiotic dependence – or interdependence – of mother and daughter. Then, there is a movement toward separation and individuation with all the complex symbolic struggles, pain, and suffering which that involves. It is a more emotional tale than many, and one goes from tears to joy as the goose girl struggles along her way. The tale can be taken as an individuation struggle, as a girl emerges into full womanhood; or it can be seen in the light of anima development for the male. In any case, it is a deeply feminine story and brings out many aspects of the evolution of the feminine.

Initially, the scenario is entirely feminine with only the mother queen and her princess daughter. There is one brief reference to a long-dead husband (see Klein, "The Goose Girl: Images of Transformation," p. 159). As a matter of fact, the queen herself is minimally present as a personage and is mainly visible in the appurtenances she gives her daughter for the journey to the betrothed. It is stated that she loves her daughter very much, and the exaggerated panoply of goods hints of something excessive in that love. Normally, too, a queen mother would personally accompany an only daughter to her wedding, to guide and sustain her through the transition from maiden to married woman. One imagines she is so upset at losing her daughter to marriage that she stays home to nurse her narcissistic loss. The "baggage" she sends most likely represents the psyche of the mother, or to look at it another way, represents the mother complex of the daughter.

The overall mood or tone of the original scene is that of a rather primitive unconscious situation. There is an aura of the primal, undifferentiated Great Mother, the original vessel. The daughter appears to be an empty, although charming and beautiful, "puella." Nonetheless, this weak being undertakes her quest into the unknown, searching for her true identity as a woman. Considering her fragility, it is remarkable that she begins at all, and this bespeaks some urge to differentiate from within the dark feminine core of the mother/daughter world itself. Perhaps it is the longing for the Other, here in the form of a betrothed. The betrothed – the animus – exerts a numinous attraction which stems from the Self.

This longing for completion can be seen clinically in the seemingly endless flirtations with men and life that dominate a woman stuck in the puella phase. The puella attitude can lead to individuation or to chronic, fruitless turmoil. In males, a puella anima may manifest as a naive fascination with relationships, things, jobs, exotic travel – which can have a quixotic, destructive quality or can lead them, too, into the world, away from the mother.

The outer world seems not at all hospitable to the princess from the beginning. The girl, protected all her life in the moist containing darkness of the queen mother, is suddenly exposed to the harsh patriarchal sun of "the world." She constantly craves water, being herself empty, with only the second-hand substance of the mother to sustain her. She can no longer drink passively from the golden mother cup – the breast – but must lie on the earth and drink directly from the stream of life.

The three drops of blood speak of suffering, of breaking mother's heart. This emphasizes the psychological and spiritual pain that must be endured in all transformation/initiation. Both mother and daughter suffer. It is the loss/death side of every profound change. These drops of blood are symbolically crucial; as Bettelheim (1977, p. 139) states, another version of the story is actually entitled, "The Cloth with the Three Drops of Blood."

According to Neumann (1970, pp. 31–32), the three great mysteries of feminine transformation are menstruation, pregnancy, and lactation. These, he states, are the "blood mysteries": the periodic bleeding of women's moon cycle, transforming blood into a living being in pregnancy, and the mysterious creation of milk from blood that enables the new life to survive and grow. Each mystery contributes its own kind of broader awareness and wisdom. Menstruation is connected with the cycles and rhythms intrinsic in all creation. Pregnancy relates to human creativity in general – the ability to bring forth unique new life from deep within. Lactation manifests the capacity to lovingly nurture new life into differentiated form, to enable it to grow – whether it be an infant, a relationship, a work of art, or human consciousness. Women have an early initiation into these core mysteries through the natural pathway of their bodies (see Klein, p. 161).

Defloration – first intercourse – could be included as a bloody mystery. Bettelheim does so, excluding lactation. However, it would seem that those mysteries *intrinsic* to the feminine are more crucial in this stage of development. Discovering the capacity to nurture, to enhance life within and without, is more fundamental than first penetration by a male. It is these mysteries that have bonded women over the ages – including virginal women. It is necessary that the goose girl, like all women, discover the potency of being "one-in-herself," grounded in the *feminine*, before intercourse or openness to the masculine can occur in any meaningful way. Defloration is connected with loss of innocence, rather than discovery of potency.

It is interesting to note that Perceval spies three drops of blood in the snow at a crucial point in the grail legend. The drops appear from a flock of wild fowl wounded by a falcon. They signal a turning point in Perceval's development. Forgetting all about the Round Table and its knights, he falls into a trance at the sight of the blood, remembering all the wrongs he has blindly committed toward women. Soon thereafter, he must confront the "loathsome damsel" who reminds him of his bad faith to the soul. The drops are like moods which paralyze a man in all their ugliness, appearing out of nowhere, insisting that he stay still and deepen. The evolution of the goose girl can be seen as anima development in a man's individuation. The mother must be left behind for a true relationship to the feminine side of a man to develop: he must grow beyond being a "good boy"–or a heroic knight. And he must suffer and learn like the goose girl in the process.

After the drops of blood are gone, the waiting-woman has more power than ever. She takes all the appurtenances of comfort and rank from the princess, including her magical horse, and swears her to secrecy. Interestingly, Falada does not speak but *notes* everything. Whatever awareness exists in the princess is as yet passive and inarticulate–she has no access to her deeper feminine potency.

The waiting-woman, on the other hand, is a powerful, expressive figure. She seems to carry many symbolic functions. She is most apparently the dark side of a doting mother's endless waiting upon her prized only daughter. This narcissistic preoccupation paralyzes and enfeebles the child who ends up with her own narcissistic syndrome of inner void and illusions of entitlement. The princess expects that life will always "wait upon" her. She is the victim of the queen's power shadow (see Klein, p. 160).

Another dimension of the waiting-woman is initiatory and transformational. Her aggressiveness challenges the princess and shakes her out of her lethargy. In this way, the power shadow of the queen, introjected by her daughter, ultimately forces the girl to connect with her own latent vitality. The waiting-woman *does* darkly serve the purpose of maturation and transformation, as a complex passed unconsciously from mother to daughter. She is the controlling shadow of the mother which weakens and humiliates her offspring; on the other hand, she is the challenge that causes the princess to awaken to her own strength. Only through being forced to the earth by this dark woman can the girl begin to discover her own inner ground.

In the male, the waiting-woman illustrates the syndrome of endlessly expecting to be served by women, and by life in general. This often stems from the power shadow of a narcissistic mother. A man cannot be fully a man when enmeshed in this way. Eventually, as with Perceval, retributions by the inner or outer woman ground him harshly, and, hopefully, awaken him, as happened to the goose girl.

The prince fits the picture of a young man unconscious of the dark side of the feminine. He greets the waiting-woman in a totally undiscerning way, unable to tell appearance from reality (see Klein, p. 162). There is a dramatic lack of differentiation on the anima level. Could this be due to the grip of an overidealized dead mother? Has he been too much in the king's shadow? It is not clear from the story. He does seem like a sort of male version of the goose girl, although his evolution is not elaborated. One gets the sense that he is unready for relationship . . . another problem for the goose girl in the future!

The king, however, shows signs of awareness from the start. He is somehow suspicious of the situation. It is noteworthy that it is he who first asks the goose girl *who she is*. The king shows wisdom, curiosity, and activity. He shows creativity by assigning her to tend the geese with Conrad, as if sensing she is not ready to cope with a full-fledged man. In this respect, the creative masculine enhances the further evolution of the feminine by a thoughtful discernment that does not act clumsily or arbitrarily but with subtle discretion. It is the sort of masculine attitude that is wise enough to respect and encourage organic feminine development.

The princess, after contact with the king, is able to actively initiate action for the first time: she pays to have Falada's head nailed up in the gateway. By paying, she is not passively served. It is also noteworthy that it is only after this act of decapitation that the horse speaks. Until then, it, too, had been entirely passive.

Detaching the head from the body has two main aspects. The first and most obvious is sacrifice and differentiation of consciousness. The "lower" part, representing the darker unconscious side of things, has been painfully separated. When things are separated, they can be seen for what they are (see Klein, p. 163). There is the possibility of greater psychological freedom. No longer must life be contained in the body-vessel of the primordial mother. There is an upward movement to head and gate, signifying increasing consciousness. Falada can now have a voice, no longer just passively observing. Suffering is now articulated, and further development is possible.

Another aspect of this horse's head is its resemblance to a hobby horse, an artificial horse's head and neck in miniature, placed on a pole a few feet long. It is then "ridden" in a jaunty fashion. Such horses are common in children's play in the Western world and have a widespread ritual significance in parts of Asia and Central America. Generally, they have an earthy, sensual, rather phallic quality. They are often associated with carnivals and weddings as a kind of teasing masculine force with erotic overtones. The male "riders" bounce and toss the head and neck in a noisy, cocky fashion. Sometimes there is a mock pursuit of the women onlookers. Altogether they contribute a mood of Dionysian revelry.

St. Augustine once forbade "the filthy practice of dressing up like a horse or stag." The hobby horse must be connected with a chthonic masculine force that was the opposite of Augustine's body-hating, overly lofty spirituality.

It is this active, earthy creativity that is being raised to consciousness in this story. Without conscious connection to such elemental life, the princess would remain a puella, endlessly flirting with dark earthy vitality in a vicarious way, manifesting in destructive relationships, always falling victim in the end. She would be unprepared for a true marriage, remaining the tool of king or prince.

Falada's head is placed in the passage between town and field, between the patriarchal and matriarchal realms, as a sort of mediator. There is a strong ritualistic sense in the passage and repetitions. The horse's words are similar to the three drops of blood, i.e., breaking the mother's heart, but here there is a consciously sought dialogue, a purposiveness in the goose girl's actions.

When she finally enters the fields of Mother Nature and her geese, she becomes empowered. Conrad, a little phallic lad, tries to steal her hair. In the realm of magic, if one possesses the part—here, the hair—one possesses the whole.

Little Conrad is a threat to her consciousness, represented by her head and hair, as well as carrying overtones of the erotic. In such situations, clinically, the puella has a dangerous potential for a wild destructive dance with a demon lover. One often sees a chronic drama of such infatuations. Multiple wild and disappointing loves, possession by wild emotions, or union with the death-lover in suicide are all too common.

But the goose girl is prepared by all she has experienced. It is Conrad who loses his head, as she summons the wind to blow his hat away. Here she demonstrates that she can utilize the elemental rhythms of nature by weaving a spell. This signifies conscious connection with the powers of the transforming feminine. She weaves her spell, and then weaves her hair, showing her newly won prowess and her self-possession. She is becoming fully empowered as a woman, nearly ready for a true marriage. No longer does she passively succumb to her own dark dependency, or to the controlling waiting-women of the world. The challenge of the waiting-woman has helped her to discover her true nature and ground. Coping with Conrad, a sort of preliminary animus figure, furthers and deepens this development.

The geese themselves are not discussed in the tale, but one is constantly aware of their background presence. After all, the tale is called "The *Goose* Girl!" All farm people know of the aggressive and territorial nature of geese: they are better watchdogs than watchdogs. Their long phallic necks ("goosing") and mythological association with Aphrodite show eros qualities. Like all swamp birds, they are strongly connected symbolically with the mother rivers and their prolific environs. In some mythologies, the goose is a world-creator, layer of the Divine Egg. In Egypt, geese were connected with spiritual transformation and immortality. The wild goose in its migratory flight is a familiar symbol of the intrinsic direction and purpose within nature, of individuation and the transcendent Self.

All these qualities are contained in the goose, and at this point in the tale, this deep archetypal ground of feminine being has replaced the original, narcissistically dominating mother complex. The fields are open and friendly, and experimentation and growth can freely take place. The goose girl can experience her own powers and leave the realm of girlhood.

The old king again manifests conscious discrimination and justice, the positive masculine that works in harmony with the feminine mysteries. Conrad, perhaps also a part of the shadow element of the patriarchy, reports his problems to the king. His curiosity is aroused, but he does not act precipitously and carefully takes in all the events of passageway and field.

When the goose girl returns home, he questions her, but she sticks to her oath of secrecy. This is a sign of her growing inner substance and integrity. She does not break down helplessly in the king's arms at first opportunity, but by her poise shows she has become a more mature woman with a respect for transcendent powers and a sense of the responsibilities of an adult. No longer must she be served, at the impulsive need of the moment. What had been narcissistic void has been filled from within by the feminine Self. This reflects another important developmental milestone.

It is fascinating how the king resolves the problem. He abandons a linear, "masculine" interrogation and relinquishes the foreground to the iron stove-vessel. Practically speaking, this gets around her oath, since she had sworn to tell no *creature*. More importantly, the stove represents the primordial creative vessel of the feminine transformation mysteries–contained heat and energy in the service of new creation. It shifts the perspective from law and order to life, to the principle of organic evolution. For life to evolve, the truth must come out–but only in a way in which both masculine and feminine are respected (see Klein, p. 164).

The goose girl is then fully accepted as the true princess. Her long inner preparation has prepared her for outer recognition. She can be clothed as the person she is and assume her rightful place in the outer world, now that she is inwardly ready. In the final meeting, it is the waiting-woman who is the unconscious one. She prescribes her own fate, which is harsh.

This final denouement illustrates the true nature and origins of the waiting-woman. She is placed in a barrel-vessel studded with nails, which represents her kinship with the negative mother who has controlling claws and devouring teeth. Falada has been part of the princess's salvation, and horses are part of the waiting-woman's destruction. They represent the passionate dynamism of life which can create or destroy. There is archetypal justice as the waiting-woman is returned to her source in a homeopathic resolution of the story.

One can, as mentioned above, take this tale as an individuation parable for men or women. The basic motif–emergence from the embrace of material overprotectiveness–is highly relevant for both sexes. The princess, so empty at first, develops a deep sense of her own essence. She finds a fertile voice: the power of nature and the ability to utilize those energies. The earthy territoriality and sense of purpose of the goose become hers. All this is recognized and affirmed by the king, the creative masculine.

Originally, the princess was unprepared to maintain her individuality in the face of the masculine element. She was unready for any relationship, much less marriage. At the end, she is sure of herself as a woman deeply connected to the feminine ground of life. It is the rather naive prince who seems likely to have trouble maintaining his autonomy in the future! In this sense, the tale seems almost a harbinger of the future, as women seem to be rediscovering the feminine Self, while men seem confused and estranged from their natures.

To see this story in terms of masculine individuation, the original picture would be a man with a capricious moodiness, constantly immersed in his own vapid hypersensitivity. Dominated by the mother complex, such a man is incapable of sustained creative effort or deep relationship with a woman. His relationship to the anima is unconscious, locked in the grip of the dark mother. He can only be "good," not truly vital or creative. In thrall to the mother complex, he has no true masculine stance until, paradoxically, he can relate to the feminine soul. Being in essence so close to the earth and the Dionysian mysteries, the positive anima can save a man from remaining forever an overspiritualized "nice boy" or a brittle warrior.

The waiting-woman reflects a man's dark moodiness, the "loathsome damsel" of his depression and irritability when his soul is subordinated to the mother's power drive. It is interesting to note parenthetically the princess's thirst, echoing dipsomania, which hits at the alcoholic tendencies often intertwined with anima problems – and often seen in the puella. The problems, the moods, can be a stimulus toward individuation for the male. He can take it as a challenge to break his dependency on the mother and develop a truly individual relationship to the feminine, and to women.

Such development in the man requires the judgment and discrimination of the king. He must be able to know the true bride from the false, real emotional meaning from transient moods and whims. It requires also the conscious acceptance of suffering as a necessary part of evolution, as epitomized in the death and resurrection of Falada. A reborn, fertile, Dionysian sense of horseplay is essential to the masculine psyche, else the man remains forever an effete nonentity at the core, his soul paralyzed in the grip of the negative mother.

The evolved goose girl as anima endows a man with an earthy masculinity that is close to nature and organic order, closer to the animal powers than the mechanical. The archetypal feminine can endow the male psyche with many gifts such as creativity and the capacity to nourish and transform. Ultimately it can lead to that greatest gift which is wisdom (Sophia).

Whatever the perspective – male or female, masculine or feminine – this moving tale of the goose girl has a distinct relevance for our own times, whether for the healing of the grail king or for the return of the goddess.

REFERENCES

Bettelheim, Bruno. 1977. *The Uses of Enchantment*. New York: Alfred A. Knopf.

Campbell, Joseph. 1983. *The Way of the Animal Powers*. San Francisco: Harper and row.

Eisler, Riane. 1987. *The Chalice and the Blade*. San Francisco: Harper and Row.

Grimm Brothers. 1973. *Grimm's Fairy Tales*. New York: The Viking Press.

Heuscher, Julius E. 1974. *A Psychiatric Study of Myths and Fairy Tales*. Springfield: Charles C. Thomas.

Jung, C. G. 1948. The phenomenology of the spirit in fairy tales. *CW* 9i:207–254. Princeton, N.J.: Princeton University Press, 1971.

Jung, Emma, and von Franz, Marie-Louise. 1971. *The Grail Legend*. London: Hodden and Stoughton.

Neumann, Erich. 1970. *The Great Mother*. Princeton, N.J.: Princeton University Press.

Sjöö, Monica, and Mor, Barbara. 1987. *The Great Cosmic Earth Mother*. San Francisco: Harper and Row.

von Franz, Marie-Louise. 1970. *An Introduction to the Psychology of Fairy Tales*. New York: Spring Publications.

______. 1972. *Problems of the Feminine in Fairy Tales*. New York: Spring Publications.

"The Goose Girl" Images of Individuation

Lucille Klein

The structure of a fairy tale frequently follows the structure that Jung perceived in dreams. Both arise from the unconscious and reveal by images what is happening in the interaction between consciousness and the unconscious. The typical form consists of four parts: the setting, the development of the plot, the culmination, and the solution (Jung 1948, pars. 561–564).

Alchemy also described the processes of the union of consciousness and the unconscious by stages. First comes the *nigredo*, the blackening phase, which is a period of confusion and disorientation. Next comes the *albedo*, the whitening phase, experienced as a stage of beginning clarity. The third phase is the *rubedo*, the reddening phase, characterized as an intense emotional period. At last comes the golden period, the *multiplicatio*, described as being constantly in the Tao, in the middle between the opposites (Jung 1944, par. 564, 1955/1956, par. 462; von Franz 1970, p. 10). This gold of the alchemists was the union of all opposites in the center, resulting in the many fruits of creativity.

In "The Goose Girl" we can follow the progress of the union of consciousness and the unconscious by observing the images and noting the stages of the movement in the story. It can be seen as a tale of the transformation of the feminine principle, both in men and women. In this process, the ego becomes humbled and relativized as missing parts of the personality are united with consciousness. Outwardly, in a woman, the story can be viewed as the transition from maidenhood to womanhood. Inwardly, it is an experience of the integration of the animus. The man can experience this process as the transformation of his relationship to his feeling side (anima) and outwardly as a growth in his ability to have a mutual relationship with a woman.

In order for these changes to take place, the truth about one's self needs to be faced. Repressions and previously split-off material have to be integrated into consciousness. Also newly emerging contents from the psyche are to be assimilated into consciousness.

This story will be amplified from the standpoint of the psychological development of the feminine principle which exists in both men and women. The particular stage of this emotional change is from adolescence to maturity. This is a problem for many people today who may remain arrested at this liminal point. Biological age does not always coincide with emotional age. Reading or hearing the tale creates the possibility that maturation will be furthered.

The Goose Girl

An old queen, whose husband was dead, had a beautiful daughter who was betrothed to a prince in a distant kingdom. When the princess was leaving for the marriage, the queen gave her many valuable items, all suitable for a royal dowry. Among the wedding gifts was an especially beautiful golden cup, for the queen loved her daughter with all her heart. A waiting-maid was also given to the princess to accompany her and deliver her safely into the hands of the bridegroom. While both the princess and the waiting-maid were given horses for the journey, the princess's horse, Falada, could talk.

At the hour of departure, the mother went to her bedroom and cut her finger with a knife. Three drops of blood fell on a white handkerchief the queen had placed under her finger. The queen then gave the handkerchief to the princess, cautioning her to take good care of it, for she would need it on the journey. As they said goodbye to each other, the princess stuck the handkerchief in her bosom.

After riding for awhile, the princess became thirsty. She asked the maid to get down from her horse, go to the stream, and bring her some water in her golden cup. The maid replied, "You go lie down over the stream to drink, for I don't want to serve you." As the princess drank from the stream she was filled with self-pity, saying, "Poor me." The three drops of blood replied, "Poor princess. If your mother could see you, her heart would break in two."

The princess was silent as she remounted her horse and rode until she became thirsty again. When they approached the next stream, the princess again asked the waiting-maid to go get her some water in her golden cup. The waiting-maid repeated her words to the princess to go lie down and drink from the stream. While the princess was drinking, the handkerchief, with the three drops of blood on it, fell out of her bosom and was carried away down stream. Although the princess was not aware, the waiting-maid gloated when she saw the handkerchief fall. Now the waiting-maid had the authority, for the princess was helpless without the three drops of blood. Immediately the waiting-maid took the royal clothes and the talking horse, Falada, telling the princess to wear the rags and to ride the nag. Also, being threatened with death, the princess had to swear that she would not tell anyone at court about these happenings. However, Falada saw and remembered everything.

As they arrived at the royal palace, the prince led the waiting-maid upstairs, thinking that she was the true bride. The princess was introduced to the king as someone who had been picked up along the way. When the king was asked to give the princess some work to do, he assigned her to help Conrad, the boy who tended the geese.

To keep the truth concealed, the waiting-maid asked the prince to have Falada's head cut off, saying the horse had caused her trouble. When the princess heard the news of these preparations, she secretly gave the knacker a gold coin to nail Falada's head over the gateway.

The next morning as the princess passed under the gate with Conrad and the geese, she said to the head, "Oh, poor Falada, hanging there." The head replied, "Oh, poor princess, how sad! If your mother knew, her heart would break in two." Then the princess and Conrad drove the geese through the fields to the meadow. There the princess sat down, undoing her golden hair to comb and braid it. Conrad, attracted to the golden hair glistening in the sunlight, tried to grab a few strands of hair for himself. The princess called on the wind to send Conrad chasing his hat by blowing it here and there into the fields. When Conrad returned with his hat, he was angry to discover that the hair of the princess was now back up in a bun and he could not get a single strand.

The next day the same events were repeated at the gate and in the meadow. When Conrad and the princess returned in the evening, Conrad went to the king to say he did not want to tend geese with that girl anymore. To the king's question as to why not, the geeseherd described what took place at the gate and in the meadow. The old king ordered Conrad to go out the next day as usual with the princess and the geese.

In the morning the king himself, hiding near the dark gateway, heard the princess talk to Falada's head. The king also followed the princess and Conrad to the meadow where he hid behind a bush. Then the king saw everything happen just as Conrad had told him. That evening the king called the goose girl to him to ask why she did all those things. She replied that she had sworn, under the threat of death, not to reveal any of her sorrows to anyone.

Since the king could get nothing out of her, he told her to crawl into the cast-iron stove to pour out all her troubles. As he went away the princess crawled into the cast-iron stove, weeping and wailing, saying, "Oh, here I am, abandoned by the whole world even though I am the daughter of a king. Since a false waiting-maid has forced me to give her my royal clothes, she has taken my place with the bridegroom. Now I live as a goose girl doing menial work. If my mother could see all of this, her heart would break."

Because the old king was standing near by, listening, he heard all that she said. The king told the princess to come out of the stove to be dressed in royal clothes and restored to her rightful place. When the son of the old king was summoned to view his true bride, he rejoiced to see her beauty and virtue. At the banquet, to which all the people were invited, the bridegroom sat at the head of the table, with the princess on one side of him and the waiting-maid on the other. Since the princess was so dazzling in her appearance, the waiting-maid did not recognize her.

At the end of the feasting and drinking, the king asked the waiting-maid a riddle: "What punishment would a woman deserve who had deceived her lord in a certain way," relating the story as he had heard it from the princess. The false bride replied, "That person should be stripped of her clothing and shut up, completely naked, in a barrel lined with sharp nails. Then two white horses should be harnessed to the barrel, dragging it up and down the streets until that person is dead."

The old king told the waiting-maid that the sentence she had just pronounced was her own, for she was the woman. After the sentence was enacted, the prince married the true bride and they ruled their kingdom in peace and joy.

In the beginning is the setting. A state of unconsciousness exists, for we are shown an image of mother and daughter or queen and princess, without the king, the father principle, the logos. Although the king as an image is being shown as one who has long been dead, he is restored at the end of the story, which reminds us that something dead can be resurrected. What had previously been lost can be restored as death and resurrection take place. The queen represents the dominant collective attitude toward the feminine, the cultural feminine ideal. She is the nurturing and protecting person, one who, in this story, carries the feeling function and the quality of relatedness, eros. The princess represents the ego, within which the budding feminine principle unfolds. Here the task of the princess is to separate from the fusion with the mother in order to develop her own femininity. She does this by finding the inner masculine, the logos principle. When a woman unites with the inner masculine, learning how to integrate it, she truly becomes a woman. Conversely, when a man unites with and relates to his feminine feeling side, he truly becomes a mature person. In identity with the mother, there is a *participation mystique* in operation, and the daughter has to discover who she is as a separate personality.

The process of individuation is set in motion by the mother as she prepares her daughter to travel to a distant kingdom (the unconscious) to marry a king's son. The second stage of the tale develops the plot as the queen gives the princess "all manner of precious things," including a goblet, a waiting-maid, and a talking horse, Falada. The mother tries to protect her daughter by also giving her a snippet of white cloth on which are three drops of the mother's blood, obtained by cutting her finger with a knife. The daughter is warned to "take good care of this." As we note these objects we need to reflect on their symbolism.

The goblet, the golden cup, symbolizes the grasp of the true situation. Consciousness is viewed collectively as golden and the cup is a container for the water of life, for the truth. Since gold is a symbol of the goal of the individuation process, in this fairy tale, the golden cup can refer to grasping something in a feminine way (von Franz 1977, p. 45).

The waiting-maid is the opposite principle but the same sex as the daughter. This aspect is commonly referred to as the shadow, a negative part of the mother which she gives to her daughter. To have power over the waiting-maid (shadow), to order her around, is an example of the attitude of the princess (ego) toward the unconscious which needs to be changed. Consciously the princess is oriented toward eros, toward love, but unconsciously she is controlled by the power drive as represented by the waiting-maid. Since the unconscious shows us the same face we show it, this attitude of wanting to control is to be made conscious and integrated. Jung has said, "Where love reigns, there is no will to power; and where the will to power is paramount, love is lacking. The one is but the shadow of the other" (Jung 1943, par. 78).

The horse is a symbol of the instinctual energy on which the ego rides without being aware of it. Behind the image of the horse is the Self which evokes the urge to individuation, the strongest instinct of all, first appearing as an animal (von Franz, 1974, pp. 259–260). The talking horse is an image of how the instincts speak with us. Since the horse is an image of the psychic energy, it is our connection with the source, with the mother, the unconscious. The instincts here needing to be integrated are sexuality and aggression.

The white piece of cloth on which there are three drops of blood gives us a powerful image. The white and red together show us a promise of what will take place in the process, the union of the feminine and the masculine. The alchemical stages of the *rubedo* (red) and the *albedo* (white) are also symbolized by this image. Following an initial black state (depression), the process will move the ego through a period of whitening (clarification) and then to an intense emotional state known as the reddening. The promise of attainment of the Self is shown in the gold of the cup and the gold of the princess's hair.

Soon after the princess and the waiting-maid begin their journey, the princess orders the waiting-maid to get her some water in her golden cup. When the waiting-maid refuses to serve her, we have the beginning of the reversal of the shadow over the ego. The princess has to lie down on the ground to drink from the brook without the cup as a container. She is slowly being humbled as she puts her bosom to the earth. She feels sorry for herself and the three drops of blood mirror her self-pity. The next time she lies on the ground to drink, she carelessly loses the white cloth with the blood which her mother had given to her. The cloth is a transitional object substituting for her mother. In losing the cloth, she has lost her conscious bond with her mother. The waiting-maid sees the cloth fall and gloats, for now she knows she has power over the princess who "without the drops of blood, became weak and helpless." Now the shadow reversal over the ego is in effect. The mother had tried to protect her daughter by giving her own blood, *pars pro tota*, but the daughter has to go through her own transformation process. The three drops of blood signify the three great sacrifices a woman makes in order to reach sexual maturity. These three are menstruation, the first intercourse, and giving birth. The sacrifices, or transformations, are sometimes called the blood mysteries, including a fourth one, lactation (Neumann 1955, pp. 31–32). However, in this story, with its emphasis on the symbolism of the pain and suffering one goes through to unite with the unconscious, it seems that first sexual intercourse is more applicable. The princess is initiated into the process of being aware of an Other by her interactions with the waiting-maid, Conrad, and the king. All three represent unconscious parts of herself that need to be integrated. To put it symbolically, they are parts of herself that penetrate into consciousness. One has to "bleed" before psychological transformation can take place. Her mother cannot do it for her and the princess has to face the trials of life on her own.

The losing of the cloth is something that the princess has to do in order to develop, to become a person in her own right. In unconscious identity with the mother, the ego is inflated and needs to be humbled and differentiated. The ego needs to learn to relate to the images presented rather than be lost in identity. In the individuation journey, the shadow is the first image from the unconscious with which the ego has to be reconciled. Realization of the shadow will free the ego from an infantile attitude and from an abnormal dependence on the parents (Jung 1943, par. 88). People who do not know enough about their own dark side are the ones most likely to fall victim to evil influences. If one knows about one's own evil possibilities, it is easier to recognize them in others. The only way to walk through the world free of being naive and foolish, one who is always protected by mother from the evils of the world, is to face the depths of one's own evil (von Franz 1977, p. 8). When the princess is not aware of her own power drive, she is taken over by it, personified as the waiting-maid. This is a common theme in fairy tales; in the encounter with the unconscious, the ego is frequently confused, disoriented, or else goes to sleep as in "Sleeping Beauty" and "Psyche and Eros." The alchemists call this experience the *nigredo*, the first stage of the work. In psychopathology, this experience is diagnosed as dysthymia, or depressive neurosis. Yet this period of melancholia, the experience of realizing the opposites within one's self, is necessary for it leads to the ultimate phase of the work, the *hieros gamos* or union of opposites (Jung 1944, par. 43).

Although the princess has lost a sense of conscious identity, Falada sees all and takes good note. The instinctual side registers what is taking place and stores it. The princess has to swear not to tell anyone of this reversal but the horse knows and can talk. With the waiting-maid's mounting of Falada and the princess's mounting of the nag, we have an image of the regression of consciousness and the progression of the unconscious. These two dynamics provide the energy for the transformation process.

When the princess and the waiting-maid arrive at the palace, the enantiodromia reaches its ultimate as the prince departs with the waiting-maid. The third phase of the drama is now in effect as we have reached the culmination or the ups and downs of the process. The prince first unites with the waiting-maid, the shadow. This union is necessary because the idealized animus, the prince, needs to become humanized through the meeting with the shadow. At the same time, the princess is placed with Conrad, the trickster animus, to complete the quarternio. In this image we see that when a woman first becomes aware of the animus, he frequently comes as a young boy. As she starts to think, her thoughts often "trick" her.

The false bride asks that Falada's head be cut off for she fears that the truth will be told. The princess initiates a turning in the process, becoming active for the first time, when she speaks up by asking that the head be preserved and nailed to the dark gateway. The head being cut off is an image of the dismemberment the ego suffers through to be transformed. The princess is cut off from the source, the body, and her thoughts are "nailed down," going nowhere. She feels sorry for herself and talks to herself. She feels hopeless and helpless, for there seems to be no way out of her predicament. She is in a stagnant situation, a state which can last a very long time on the initiation journey. She cannot help herself; yet, as she gives up the attitude of thinking she is in control of the unconscious, the unconscious will also give up its attempt to dominate her (Jung 1952, par. 671).

Although the princess is in a stuck place, she is very courageous. She is assigned to help the geeseherd, Conrad, tend the geese. After the encounter with the shadow, there is a confrontation with the animus. Conrad represents an immature stage of integrating the thinking function, the logos. Consciousness and the unconscious go through a stage of tricking each other. When he tries to grasp her hair, she tricks him by having his cap blown away. It is as though we have an image of her having a saving thought as she summons the wind. Combing her hair is an image of straightening out the thoughts in her head. Here is the beginning of the *albedo*, the whitening. As she sits there combing her hair, she is beginning to focus and reflect. Things begin to get a little clearer. Her golden hair is an image of her great worth. Letting down her golden hair and caring for it is an image of the realization and valuing of her sexual maturity and a way of recognizing her worth as an individual woman. She is becoming independent and mature. She is capable of enduring the reversal and is not destroyed in the process (Stein 1986). She does not allow her immature animus to destroy her self-worth. At this point she is capable of withstanding the boy's anger where previously she surrendered to the waiting-maid's anger.

The geese she tends can also be symbols of immature thoughts for which she needs to care. Geese are sometimes considered stupid, for they will follow one another into disaster. However, she is on the ground, in the middle realm between air and water. Caring for the geese is also a symbol of getting grounded, free of her "airy" thoughts. In this middle place, she is also achieving a balance between the inflation/deflation upheaval she has been going through. Since the goose is a sacred animal of Aphrodite's, to tend geese also shows an emphasis on valuing sexuality. The goose has been an erotic symbol for both sexes; it was the bird of creation that laid the Golden Egg. When the goose was carved on tombstones, it stood for marital love. Geese are a symbol of sexual union and conjugal fidelity as there is a common belief that geese mate for life.

The horse's head over the dark gateway is an image of death and resurrection. The horse's head, although "dead," is living still in that it speaks. The gate on which the head is placed is a symbol of the entrance to the unconscious; the libido regresses back to the source and is "born again." The head separated from the body is a symbol of the longing to return to the protection of the mother, a longing that needs to be sacrificed. It is time now for the regression to end. The gate is also an image of the middle realm, an entrance to the country on one side and the city on the other. As she goes back and forth through the gate we get a feeling of the union of nature and spirit.

By refusing to allow Conrad to steal her hair, she frustrates him so much that he complains to the king. The princess refuses to tell her secret to the king in order to keep the oath she made under the open sky. The king shows respect for her integrity and makes no attempt to lure her away from her decision. Instead he persuades her to tell her truth to the cast-iron stove, which is similar to talking in an analytic or therapeutic vessel (Zahner-Roloff 1979). She goes through a period of incubation as she climbs in and tells her story in a safe place. The stove is an image of transformation; in the cooking process, food is transformed from one state to another. Her affects are allowed to come to full expression as she gives vent to her emotions in the telling of her story. The alchemical state of the *rubedo*, the reddening, is coming to pass.

The king listens and learns the truth. He restores the persona by dressing the princess in her royal garments. Next he brings her to her proper place as he informs his son of the true bride, thereby fulfilling the function of the logos principle. Now the king asks the waiting-maid to mete out her own punishment as we come to the fourth part of the drama, the solution or the result that will take place. This action reminds us of another meaning of the goose. The goose represents a special aspect of Mother Nature called Nemesis, meaning to distribute or attribute to each one what she has coming to her from the way she has lived her life. It is an unconscious principle by which everyone gets what they deserve. The waiting-maid states that when a person usurps the place of another, the usurper should be put to death by being dragged in a nail-studded vessel until dead (Bettelheim 1977, p. 140). This image reminds us of the devouring mother who appears when we refuse to grow up.

The king orders that the sentence be carried out and once this is done, the *hieros gamos* takes place as the young king and the right bride are married: "and they ruled the kingdom together in peace and happiness." The image of the king, who was absent in the beginning of our story, is present and saves the princess at the end. She is delivered by the father from the unconscious. In the marriage of the prince and princess, consciousness and the unconscious are united and the threshold between maidenhood and womanhood is crossed. The golden state of consciousness is now prevalent and the center of the personality resides in the Self.

This story presents the Jungian individuation process in a nutshell. On this journey of initiation, the unconscious contents are joined with the ego. This voyage to find a missing part is repeated over and over in order to become whole. The two halves separated here are the feminine and masculine, or the feeling function and the thinking function. The need and the longing to unite are described in such a profound way that one experiences the separation and the union of the opposites. The suffering and the pain caused by the loss of identity with the maiden is clear, yet identities must be lost or given up as we mature.

The major theme in the story is the truth that in order to individuate one must grow up. One needs to let go of former identities and awaken to possibilities of change in the personality so that new potentialities can be developed. When the call to individuate is ignored, destruction will take place. The energies that are pressing for integration will turn destructive if they are denied the value and attention they require. When these needed changes are accepted, growth and transformation result.

REFERENCES

Bettelheim, Bruno. 1977. *The Uses of Enchantment*. New York: Vintage Books.

Jung, C. G. 1943. On the psychology of the unconscious. *CW* 7:1–119. Princeton, N.J.: Princeton University Press, 1966.

______. 1944. *Psychology and Alchemy*. In *CW*, vol. 12. Princeton, N.J.: Princeton University Press, 1968.

______. 1948. On the nature of dreams. *CW* 8:28–297. Princeton, N.J.: Princeton University Press, 1969.

______. 1952. *Symbols of Transformation*. In *CW*, vol. 5. Princeton, N.J.: Princeton University Press, 1967.

______. 1955/1956. *Mysterium Coniunctionis*. *CW*, vol. 14. Princeton, N.J.: Princeton University Press, 1970.

Neumann, Erich. 1955. *The Great Mother*. Princeton, N.J.: Princeton University Press.

Stein, Murray. 1986. Personal conversation, February 12.

von Franz, Marie-Louise. 1970. *A Psychological Interpretation of the Golden Ass of Apuleius*. Zurich: Spring Publications.

______. 1974. *Shadow and Evil in Fairy Tales*. New York: Spring Publications.

______. 1977. *Individuation in Fairy Tales*. Zurich: Spring Publications.

Made in the USA
Las Vegas, NV
27 April 2025

21434384R00104